ENDORSEMENTS

I am intrigued by the title of Kerry Kirkwood's new book, *Accessing the Blessing of Heaven's Currency.* I liked it so much that Kerry has a show on ISN Network with a similar title, *The Currency of Heaven.* I am convinced that none of us have fully tapped into all the currency that is deposited in our heavenly accounts. Kerry is showing us how we can deposit and spend heavenly currency to see miracles released in these last days of glory.

Sid Roth
Host of *It's Supernatural*

I was captured by the first paragraph of Kerry's new book. He speaks of the burden of the Lord that was upon Habakkuk and how he had a similar burden on him in regards to his book, *Accessing the Blessing of Heaven's Currency.* God spoke to the prophet and told him to, *"write the vision and make it plain, that they may run who read it."* One of the translations gives us this insight into the burden of the Lord; it means that he had the highest desire for the people of God. In all the years I have known Kerry Kirkwood, I have never heard him speak or had a conversation with him that I was not encouraged by his life message. Everything he says or does is with the highest desire for the people of God. This book is a classic in regard to the legacy of his life which is yet to be spent. Each chapter will help you recognize and understand like Kerry, you have more in the storeroom than you do in the showroom. I appreciate authors who help me to think, and in this book Kerry makes me think. I call this a good read and it has content in it that you can take to the Bank of Heaven.

Cleddie Keith
Senior Pastor, Heritage Fellowship

This man of God is giving a teaching you can trust. The revelation he is releasing will produce miraculous results! Get ready for transformations and manifestations from Heaven!

Pastor Tony Kemp
President of the Acts Group

ACCESSING *the* BLESSING *of* HEAVEN'S CURRENCY

DESTINY IMAGE BOOKS
BY KERRY KIRKWOOD

Accessing the Blessing of Heaven's Currency

The Power of Imagination

The Power of Blessing

The Power of Right Thinking

Pursue, Overtake, Recover

The Secret Power of Covenant

KERRY KIRKWOOD

ACCESSING *the* BLESSING *of* HEAVEN'S CURRENCY

Withdrawing Power from Your
Heavenly Account for
Answered Prayers

DESTINY IMAGE® PUBLISHERS, INC.
P.O. Box 310, Shippensburg, PA 17257-0310
"Publishing cutting-edge prophetic resources to super-naturally empower the body of Christ"

This book and all other Destiny Image and Destiny Image Fiction books are available at Christian bookstores and distributors worldwide.

For more information on foreign distributors, call 717-532-3040.

Reach us on the Internet: www.destinyimage.com.

ISBN 13 TP: 978-0-7684-7387-2

ISBN 13 eBook: 978-0-7684-7388-9

ISBN 13 HC: 978-0-7684-7439-8

ISBN 13 LP: 978-0-7684-7438-1

For Worldwide Distribution, Printed in the U.S.A.

1 2 3 4 5 6 7 8 / 27 26 25 24 23

DEDICATION

I DEDICATE this book to all of the churches that have invited me to share the truths in this book, *Accessing the Blessing of Heaven's Currency*. It was through many of you prompting me to continue on this trek of research, requesting even more teaching coming from this research.

I also dedicate this book to the many gifted authors who have blazed the trail toward the medium of books and literature.

I give special thanks to my own congregation, Trinity Fellowship in Tyler, Texas, that has been an active laboratory for this project. It was through your excitement and participation in the application of this teaching that convinced me to share with a larger audience. Trinity Fellowship, you share in the writing of this book.

Now to my family of whom I am very proud: Kevin, Casey, Kristen, and Kara. It is very rewarding to hear of your love for God and determined faith you are now imparting to your children, our grandchildren. One of the true joys of my heart was when I was told my oldest granddaughter, Genevieve, had read my fourth book, *The Power of Right Thinking*, at age 11. She went on to take it to school for "Show and Tell." She encourages me to keep writing for the legacy we will leave behind. Love you, Genevieve Kirkwood!

For all who read this book and find it to be a valuable tool for breakthrough living, I am thankful for your hunger for more.

ACKNOWLEDGMENTS

L IKE any project of this size, it takes a team to push it across the finish line. My wife, Diane, was the biggest cheerleader of the team who always encouraged me; and when other things got in the way, she would remind me to stay focused. Her affirmation means more to me than any I have received. This is my sixth book—and as every book is different in writing, this one flowed different from any of the others. I felt the Holy Spirit speaking all through the book as I wrote, prompting thoughts and Scripture that I had not used in The Currency of Heaven teaching series.

I am blessed with an awesome team of pastors surrounding me and supporting me through this process. When I needed time to finish, they were understanding and covered any pastoral duties that needed attention. I am thankful for Pastor Duane Hett, our executive pastor who is known for keeping everything running smoothly and was a great help with software issues with the book. Our amazing office manager, Tina Smith, is the kindest person anyone could encounter. She made sure I had the time I needed to work undisturbed.

Pastor Jim Hahn, my associate, does a great job assisting me in teaching and discipling the church, I couldn't do what I do without him being who he is. Pastor Franky Benitez is not only a skilled worship leader

and speaker, he also assisted me by ensuring all my writing was saved and backed up. Alex Miller, the newest addition to the team, is awesome at understanding the youth of our day. Alex is a gift to our youth department.

I would be remiss if I didn't mention the congregation of Trinity Fellowship in Tyler, Texas, who has been an inspiration to me. Week after week they were the laboratory in which the teaching of this book was shared. Their responses to this message encouraged me to take it to the next level and inscribe it into this book for others to experience.

CONTENTS

INTRODUCTION

*The oracle (a burdensome message—a pronouncement
from God) which Habakkuk the prophet saw*
(Habakkuk 1:1 Amplified Bible).

S written in Habakkuk 1:1, the burden of the Lord was upon
the prophet Habakkuk. Beginning the next chapter we read,
*"Then the Lord answered me and said, 'Write the vision make it
plain on tablets, that he may run who reads it'"* (Habakkuk 2:2 NKJV). I
have done my best to adhere to responding similarly to the Holy Spirit.
I first felt the burden of the Lord before endeavoring to write what I
was envisioning. I waited three years to see if the burden would dissipate
or increase. Obviously since I am writing this revelation, the burden
increased rather than evaporate. I felt the accountability of the Holy
Spirt not just to have this book shut up inside me but to put it out for
others to read and run with for decades to come.

My intentions are that others will be able to expand even further into
the depths of the currency of Heaven. May you be more intentional how
you live or sow your life now for a greater effectiveness with authority
and power of the Holy Spirit. Hosea 4:6 says, *"My people are destroyed for
lack of knowledge."* This book is more connecting with Heaven to earth

right now as well as the eternal rewards to follow. There are many great books now more than ever before. This book will fine-tune the macro perspectives into micro seeing to maximize all God has placed in your account.

CONNECTING THE DOTS

The picture is still illuminated in my mind of myself as a young child of no more than 5 or 6 years of age, my nose pressed against the storefront window at Milam's Toyland in Amarillo, Texas, during the Christmas season. I was viewing a bicycle inside displayed as if it would win the Daytona 500 race. I thought to myself, *If I could only ride that bike, I wouldn't want anything else in the world.* I expressed my wish list to my mother with the negotiating idea that this would take the place of at least two or maybe three birthdays plus Christmases to come.

She quickly explained how much the bicycle cost and that it was far out of our family's range to buy. I said to her, "Just write a check, like you always do, and we could take it home today." I didn't understand the problem. She tried to explain something about having money in the bank to cover the check. Well, it didn't happen that day and I felt disappointed. With hopes dashed, I soon learned I had to have money to exchange for what I believed to be the most special bike in the world. It was a lesson I would need as I entered the future.

> For which of you, intending to build a tower, does not sit down
> first and count the cost, whether he has enough to finish it
> (Luke 14:28 NKJV).

Everything has a cost even the things that we receive for free. Someone somewhere paid a price for what we received. Understanding how the Kingdom of God works and the cost involved helped me immensely in knowing how to pray and stand for miracles. "Jesus paid it all," as the old hymn goes. There is no doubt that it's been paid, but how I apply what has been paid makes all the difference in the world. It is the difference between wishing for something and possessing it.

This book will open a spiritual account that will help you know how to release Heaven into your world. In this book you will:

- Learn how to increase your capacity for greater spiritual authority to apply toward every crisis you face—knowing you have deposited ahead of time the spiritual might to win every battle.

- Learn the various levels and values of currency and how to withdraw from what you have been sowing toward.

- Feel more confident when praying. You will see your prayers go from only asking the Father of Lights to move in your behalf, to declaring what is not appearing as though it is manifesting.

- Recognize how to partner with the Holy Spirit in directing Heaven's assets toward your victory. The Holy Spirit is the administrator over everything Jesus said to us. He reminds us of what was given to us and all that we have in our account. I believe this will be a total game changer for you as you enter a partnership with Heaven to see the manifest power of His glory come upon all you have stood steadfast to see.

I chose to title this book *Accessing the Blessing of Heaven's Currency* because it gives a clear picture of how we can access the Kingdom of God. This doesn't mean that we can buy our way in, but there are certainly keys to understanding how to engage this exchange between Heaven and earth.

In this book you will learn the various currencies and their value to activate movement regarding your prayers. Certainly, the blood of Jesus is the most valuable currency you have. And you will learn to employ this precious currency and many other types of Heaven's currency.

WHAT DETERMINES THE VALUE OF A CURRENCY?

Currency is a form of exchange for goods and services. There are many kinds of currency. There is emotional currency we expend when we are invested in relationships. There is also spiritual currency that we will explore at length in this book. Being a good steward of heavenly currency is the focus of much of what is discussed in this book and how to utilize all that we have deposited into our heavenly account.

Monetary currency is the most common use of the term; historically, monetary currency was called a note or a promissory note. It was a paper note promising to pay a stated amount to a specified person. The note was backed up by the bank so it could be exchanged for silver or gold that was in turn exchanged for food or services rendered. The bills would circulate as a form of payment. Every country has its own currency or paper notes. In and of itself the paper has no value, but what it represents is where the real value lies.

The currency of each country backs up the banks that circulate currency. The strength of that government is the extent that the currency can be trusted as a true value. The currency value is determined by the success and stability of each country. The reason the United States dollar is accepted worldwide is because of the strength of the economy and the strength of its military. If a country has a weak defense and its enemies continually threaten the stability of its government, then the currency is weak and not trusted.

What makes the currency of heaven so valuable, you ask? Well, it's the stability of the Kingdom of God. Our God has never lost a battle. Jesus' resurrection is proof without doubt that the currency can never be weakened. The army of the Host of Heaven is another sign this currency will never lose its power. When you use the name of Jesus, you are assured that Heaven is attentive and ready to react.

When I was in elementary school, I used to walk to school when the weather permitted. There was a small mom-and-pop convenience store near the school. My dad set up a credit account there for me. In the morning I would get thirty cents for the school lunch (yes you heard right, thirty cents for a full lunch), and in the afternoon on my way home I was allowed twenty-five cents to stop at the store for candy. Each time I would sign my dad's name, who would pay the bill at the end of the month.

My friends and I walked to and from school and they noticed my pattern of stopping at the store in the afternoon. One afternoon my friend followed me into the store. He saw me carefully pick out just the right amount of the penny candy, which I could buy by the piece at that time. My friend Dave followed suit and stood behind me as to follow the protocol. The owner counted my candy and wrote the amount on the ticket, and I signed my dad's name. Dave proceeded to do the same, except the owner asked him who he was. Dave said, "I want to do what

Kerry just did." The store owner glaringly looked at him and said, "I know his daddy; who is your daddy?" Well, Dave's father had not set up an account for him, so he walked out feeling slighted—until I shared my stash with him.

Are you known in Heaven? Do you have the rights of a son or daughter of God in Heaven? It's not enough to know the right protocol and the right buzz words to use; we must have an account set up by our heavenly Father. Counterfeit money or currency is an attempt to look and sound like the real thing, but the angel army will not respond because this kind of currency you don't carry in our wallet—it's printed on your heart with a seal that cannot be stolen. It is sealed by the Holy Spirit and has the approval and acceptance of the government of God.

You will discover in reading this book how powerful the government of the Kingdom of God really is and how powerful its currency is. You will also be able to discern the counterfeit currency that some try to use for their own spiritual gains. I hope you will read this book from cover to cover and discover for yourself the power and value of heavenly currency, and how to spend or use it. Heaven is ready to welcome your engagement. You will be delighted to see how the angels respond to this priceless currency.

In the natural sense, currency has influence and how we use that influence is noted by rewards of stewardship at the end of the age when we stand before the judgment seat of Christ. There is also influence with supernatural currency that calls for stewardship as well. I would not want to stand before the Lord and find out that I was given spiritual wealth and influence over demonic structures and influences in the lives of friends and family, and I chose not to spend it. Many of us are probably not even aware of this kind of access into the throne room of Heaven. Just like the young boy who had a vision for a valuable bike and counted the cost to obtain the bike, you too can develop insight for what

you desire to see as Heaven responds to what you have deposited in your account. In this book you will learn how to release on earth what has already been deposited in your heavenly account.

What began as a random search to see why some people found answers to prayers and others came up empty-handed has now become a passion in my heart. I want to discover the divine connection as to why some people have greater authority over their destiny than others. I knew there had to be a way to see more answered prayers than unanswered. I didn't believe God had His favorites and others were left out. Although I still believe God doesn't play favorites, I did discover God gives favor toward those who know and understand how to live in His Kingdom and obtain the favor of the King.

I set out to find a common denominator, or perhaps to find there was nothing linking answered or unanswered prayers at all. I know the Bible is filled with parabolic examples revealing why some results are different from others. For example, the parable of the Sower and the Seed in Matthew 13. The parable is clearly showing there were different rewards of harvest depending on the environment where the seed was sown. So this tells me there are different levels to prayer being answered.

As you will discover, there is not just one key or thing that opens the reservoirs of Heaven; but instead, there are many with varying degrees of cost and reward. Yet they all will obviously flow through the knowledge of Jesus. Proverbs 13:12 (NKJV) says, *"Hope deferred makes the heart sick, but when the desire comes, it is a tree of life."* I truly believe after reading this book and applying the currency of heavenly wisdom, fresh hope will come alive in your soul and you too will know how to invest through faith the valuable currency you have been given to see your prayers come to pass.

So, I want to ask this question as you start reading these chapters. Do you feel you are wealthy in the currency of Heaven, or do you feel undeserving of what has been deposited in your account? Genesis15:6 tells us that Abram believed the Lord, and God credited it to him as righteousness. Notice the accounting term used in Abram's account. He believed what God said and it was *"credited"* or deposited in regard to Abram's belief. I believe that when we trust and act in faith we gain credit that goes toward a greater level of spiritual wealth and authority.

What is your credit score in Heaven today? Stay tuned and plugged in to gain a larger deposit and greater spiritual understanding of spiritual currency.

Do We Really Have
A SPIRITUAL BANK
ACCOUNT IN HEAVEN?

IRST a little background. In Genesis 14:14-23, there is a powerful dialogue between God and Abram right after Abram
took trained servants of his household and rescued Lot, his
brother's son, from ten kings who had raided Sodom and had taken
his nephew captive. Melchizedek was the king of Salem and who
most scholars tell us was actually a temporary, pre-Christ incarna-
tion of God known as a Theophany or a Christophany. Melchizedek
meets Abram with bread and wine which are great symbols for the
Word and Spirit.

It's exciting to see all the Trinity represented here in this Scripture
passage, as not only agreeing in Heaven but also giving agreement on
earth (see 1 John 5:7-8). The agreement of the Three on earth is related
to us allowing the Three on earth—Word, Spirit, blood—to work
through us and with us. As you will discover further into this book,
these Three on earth finding agreement with those of faith on earth
causes a response from the Three in Heaven. Knowing how to apply the
agreement on earth causes action on earth.

Hebrews 7:15 makes the connection between Jesus and Melchizedek as a priesthood without beginning or ending and as the king of Salem. This leads me to conclude that the same blessing that was conferred by Melchizedek carries over into the New Covenant of today and becomes part of the blessing passed on to us. Melchizedek blesses Abram by saying, *"Blessed be Abram of God Most High, possessor of heaven and earth"* (Genesis 14:19 NKJV). Notice the language used, *"Abram of God,"* not God of Abram. This is confirming to us this is God declaring the blessing. The declaration of possessor of Heaven and earth makes way for Abram to have authority not only on his earthen territory but has gained access into the heavenly realm as well.

On top of that, Melchizedek gives a tithe to Abram. Tithe, or tenth, is the number of testing. There is an unusual sharing of authority by confirming it with testing of a tithe. The tithe was the sacred portion; not just any tenth, it was the first of the harvest. Prophetically God is confirming His will to Abram through giving the sacred, ratifying His promise of throne room access. In Genesis 15:1, the blessing continues by admonishing Abram that God would be his shield and great reward. Not only is God confirming his wealth and influence, He would also protect what God had given Abram.

> He took him outside and said, "Look up at the sky and count
> the stars—if indeed you can count them." Then he said to him,
> "So shall your offspring be" (Genesis 15:5 NIV).

Hang on; right when you thought it couldn't get any better, God brings Abram outside in verse 15:5 (NIV) and says to him, *"Look up at the sky and count the stars."* Note the emphasis on counting. Stars usually represent family and legacy, and God said, "If you can number the stars, that's how numerous your descendants will be." God is expanding more

than Abram could imagine since he had no children at the time. It is worth noting that God took Abram outside of where he was seeing and said, "Look up." The point being we become narrow in scope and thinking when we can only see what has always been familiar to us. God was multiplying Abram not only on earth, but also multiplying his influence in Heaven. Please don't miss this nuance in this verse.

Melchizedek said to Abram that he is a possessor of Heaven before referring to earth. This is of great importance because we can have no significant influence unless we first take hold of Heaven. Jesus gave His disciples a very specific prayer in Matthew 6:10 (NKJV) by praying, *"Your kingdom come. Your will be done on earth as it is in heaven."* Earth is to follow the direction and leadership of Heaven. It is important to understanding what Heaven is looking for on earth, to partner with earthen vessels. *"But we have this treasure in earthen vessels, that the excellency of the power may be of God, and not of us"* (2 Corinthians 4:7 NKJV).

In Genesis 15:6 is the knot that ties all this together. Abram believed in the Lord and He, God, accounted it to him for righteousness. God used the term of accounting. The apostle Paul picks up on the same revelation in Galatians 3:5-6. The Greek usage of the word *accounting* is made up of two words *logizomai,* meaning to count and do inventory (Strong's #3049). Inventory is very important from a business perspective. Your inventory is what you use to multiply and increase influence. Your inventory is what you plant to grow more inventory or seed.

From a military perspective, inventory is the assets and weapons you want to keep track of before going to war. God is showing Abram that He has made a deposit into His account in Heaven to be used to bring Heaven to earth. His influence on earth is connected to his deposits in Heaven. As a person sows, so will that person reap (2 Corinthians 9:6). Sowing into the Heaven releases fruit on earth.

We must understand that we have an account in Heaven—not just rewards given to us at the end of the age—assets we can acquire for use now on earth for the war we fight daily. To be spiritually bankrupt in Heaven leaves us vulnerable to the principalities that have dominion over certain regions of the earth.

Jesus gives us an example of various levels of authority in Mark 9:17-29. There was a man whose son was demon possessed with a mute spirit. The father cried out to Jesus for help saying that he brought his son to Him and spoke to His disciples, but they could not cast out the demon. As soon as the father brought his son to Jesus, the demons began to make the son convulse. Jesus rebuked the demon, and the spirit that afflicted the boy came out. Later Jesus was asked by His disciples why they could not cast the demon out of the boy. The disciples had been sent out by Jesus before this time with authority to cast our spirits and heal the sick so they must have had some success previously. So, they were perplexed as to why they could not free the young boy.

Jesus said to them, *"This kind* [or level of authority] *can come out by nothing but prayer and fasting"* (Mark 9:29 NKJV). Fasting is a discipline that we all should use to keep our flesh submitted to God. Demons are not afraid of us fasting, nor is God impressed by our discipline of fasting. But, fasting weakens the flesh so the Holy Spirit has greater influence over us.

My sense is that the disciples had yet to gain enough in their spiritual accounts to drive out a demon of such spiritual authority. The disciples had yet to gain the bandwidth to tackle one that been enrooted for years since the boy's childhood. The disciples would prove later to carry greater faith and authority as they overcame other obstacles. In times past kings would rule their dynasties with military might and power, and the more they conquered other kingdoms, the more powerful they became. When a king conquered the domain of another kingdom, he would take the

crown from the destroyed king and place it on his own head and ride through the streets declaring a new king was now in control. Each victory would increase the influence and dominion of his kingdom.

We gain authority through what we overcome, not what we undergo. Abram had a name change after his encounter with God—from Abram meaning father, to Abraham meaning a father of many. Many believers have a position of authority, but they have not increased their accounts to the level needed to deal with principalities of this age.

CORNELIUS' HEAVENLY ACCOUNT

Acts 10 tells us the story of Cornelius, and sets my point even deeper relating to having a depository in Heaven. Cornelius was part of the Roman occupation of the Jews. He was a centurion who showed his rank was worthy of commanding at least a hundred soldiers. The Bible describes Cornelius as a devout man, one who feared God. He also was known for directing his household with the same principles. He had the reputation of giving to the poor. Cornelius had an encounter with an angel of the Lord. When Cornelius inquired of the Lord, the angel said to him, *"Your prayers and your gifts to the poor have come up as a memorial offering before God"* (Acts 10:4 NIV). *Memorial* in the Greek is very specific: *mnémosunon,* meaning to mark for remembrance (Strong's #3422).

The three things mentioned in connection with Cornelius was for more than a passing moment. God wanted him to know there was a marked receipt in Heaven with his name on the account. The next day an angel was sent to Peter who was known to have prejudice against the Gentiles (non-Jewish people). While Peter was on the rooftop waiting

for dinner, he had a vision of animals coming down that he knew were not kosher or permitted to be eaten by Jews. Each time the Lord said to him, *"Kill and eat"* (Acts 10:13-16 NIV).

Each time Peter responded as any Jew would do, by saying, *"I have never eaten anything impure or unclean."* The Lord responded in this vision saying, *"Do not call anything impure that God as made clean"* (Acts 10:15 NIV). The vision occurred three times. By this time, the men Cornelius sent to find Peter were at Peter's house telling him he should come to Cornelius. This interaction between the angel and Cornelius drew out of his memorial or account in Heaven and brought God's response to change Peter's mindset about Gentiles—which opened the door for the Gospel to be preached among the Gentiles. It was Cornelius' account that was enlarged by his obedience to the angel of the Lord and his giving to the poor.

Many of us pray large prayers that are good, but then offer the Lord teacups to put the answers in. Perhaps the reason we don't see answers is because we have yet to enlarge our capacity to receive what we are asking for. So for many of us, the answer has yet to come until we have grown into the stature to steward that level of authority.

I hope we can see that our actions and responses to God's Word are being passed through the accounting of Heaven. The Lord keeps better books than we can. The simplest of obedience may result in greater deposits in Heaven than what we can even imagine. Just know you are known in Heaven, and you are wealthier than what you realize.

Acts 19:11-20 (NIV) is the account of some unusual miracles performed by the apostle Paul, including how his handkerchiefs or aprons healed the sick, diseases were cured, and evil spirits were expelled. There were some itinerant exorcists who took it upon themselves to call on the name of the Lord Jesus for people who had evil spirits, saying, *"In*

the name of the Jesus whom Paul preaches, I command you to come out."
The seven sons of a chief priest named Sceva also tried to drive out an
evil spirit. But the evil spirit said, *"Jesus I know, and Paul I know, but
who are you?" Then the man who had the evil spirit jumped on them and
overpowered them all. He gave them such a beating that they ran out of the
house naked and bleeding"* (Acts 19:15-16 NIV). Obviously, the sons of
Sceva and others were bankrupt when it came to exercising the heavenly
currency. Heaven knows those who belong to the Lord Jesus Christ, and
only those who know Him can use His name with power and authority.
It takes more than attending a deliverance seminar and getting a certificate to see the release of God's power.

The account you have in Heaven is directly connected to knowing
Him intimately, not just knowing about Him. Does Jesus know you?
Because the demons certainly know Him and those who are covered
with His name. John 20:22 (NKJV) says, *"And when He had said this,
He breathed on them, and said to them, 'Receive the Holy Spirit.'"* This
was certainly before the baptism of the Holy Spirit, yet there was a sort
of commissioning of them when Jesus says, *"As the Father has sent Me, so
I send you"* (John 20:21 NKJV). Even today some take this as Jesus giving them the name of His Father by breathing on them or transferring
the name of the Father into them. It would be similar to an ambassador
sent from his or her country to represent the will and messaging of their
government to another country.

Soon after this, the disciples not only received the authority to be
sent, but with the Acts 2 encounter with the Holy Spirit baptism, they
were empowered. The sons of Sceva went to cast out demons, but they
were representing their own interests, not the Kingdom of God. The
baptism of the Holy Spirit gave the disciples the power to do what they
were being sent to do. Along with this new baptism was the boldness
and confidence to do the work of the Kingdom of God.

We can see the transformation from authority to power in Acts 3:2-7 when Peter and John were going to the temple to pray. A lame man was at the gate called Beautiful. Interesting to note is that Beautiful is translated as the "Gate of right timing." No doubt this lame man was there regularly at his personal spot to beg for money and food. There is a good probability that this was not Peter's first time to see the infirmed man. But since receiving the baptism of the Holy Spirit, everything had changed. The apostles no longer saw the poor man as an impossibility or just felt empathy for him. They now saw him through the eyes of the Holy Spirit. With great boldness Peter commanded him to rise and walk. He was now so convinced of the power of the Holy Spirit that Peter took the man by the hand and lifted him up.

Those who were baptized with the Holy Spirit were no longer willing to just wait and see what would happen if they tried out some new teaching. No. Now they were carriers of the name Jesus imparted to them with the authority power to carry out their mission. The apostles began to draw on the currency that had been deposited for them to serve on earth as it was in Heaven. Acts 4:33 (NKJV) says, *"And with great power the apostles gave witness to the resurrection of the Lord Jesus. And great grace was upon them all."* The baptism of the Holy Spirit gave them access to the currency deposited on their behalf.

The Blood of Jesus—The Most Valuable
HEAVENLY CURRENCY

I T is obvious that the blood of Jesus is the single most important factor in the New Covenant. It is the game changer that destroyed the ownership of the devil over humankind. It was always God's plan to destroy the devil with God's own offering, His Son. This caught the devil off guard; he didn't see it coming. The blood of Jesus destroyed the bloodline of Adam and reintroduced the bloodline of the incorruptible seed, which is the Seed of Christ. Without the shedding of blood there is no remission of sin according to Hebrews 9:22.

But do you know why the blood of Jesus is the currency of Heaven? The why is equally important to release the power that is in the precious blood of Jesus. First Corinthians 2:8 (NIV) tells us: *"None of the rulers of this age understood it, for if they had, they would not have crucified the Lord of glory."*

Lucifer was cast out of the place of glory, to a planet of darkness, where he became known as the ruler, the prince of darkness. None of the angelic host were familiar with blood. They only had spiritual bodies and did not encounter flesh and blood until the creation of man. Genesis 2:7 (NKJV) says, *"And the Lord God formed man of the dust of the ground,*

and breathed into his nostrils the breath of life; and man became a living being." There were two processes at work at the creation of humankind. First, God formed (*asah*) man from the dust of the earth. The Hebrew word *asah* means to press into place much like a potter would fashion a clay vessel or to make from substance that already exists. This is where Adam gained his physical body. The second process (*brera*) refers to creating or bringing to life. Forming from the dust is to fashion from substance that was earthly or was already on the earth, whereas *brera* refers to bringing to life from substance that does not exist on earth.

When God breathed *pneuma* into man, something radically began to change. The original text says, Adam became a "speaking spirit." Adam received seed from another world known as the Kingdom of God. With that breath of God, Adam now carried the DNA of God. This takes us back to the point of the blood. God gave Adam an earthly connection to the heavenly as well as the earthly. Leviticus 17:11 (NKJV) states, *"For the life of the flesh is in the blood, and I have given it to you upon the altar to make atonement for your souls; for it is the blood that makes atonement for the soul."*

It is clear to see that if God breathed into man and gave him life and life is in the blood, then we have to conclude that the blood of Adam came from the Life or Spirit of God. Understanding how to invoke the blood of Jesus gives us influence over all things, both in Heaven and on earth. The only way Lucifer could enter humankind was through a bloodline. Through the serpent there was a broken place that allowed an infusion of sin for the first time into God's creation. God wanted Himself to be intimate in relationship with Adam. But Eve allowed an outside counterfeit to enter the relationship.

By that act of disobedience, Lucifer now infected the holy bloodline to destroy God's expression of His glory on earth. Subsequently, it had to be through blood that the bloodline could be purged and restored to an intimate relationship with our heavenly Father who originally gave us

His DNA. All of humankind was now morally bankrupt and forced to live outside the presence of Eden. There was a gap between God and man that had to be closed and restored with holy DNA or a currency that was from a pure and uncorruptible bloodline. The bloodline of Adam up through Cain had been polluted. Romans 5:9-10 (NKJV) says:

> *Much more then, having now been justified by His blood, we shall be saved from wrath through Him. For if when we were enemies we were reconciled to God through the death of His Son, much more, having been reconciled, we shall be saved by His life.*

And John 1:4-5 (NKJV) tells us, "*In Him was life, and the life was the light of men. And the light shines in the darkness, and the darkness did not comprehend it.*" Notice the connection between light and life. In Jesus is life, and the life is in the blood; also in Him was light and the light shines and the darkness could not overcome or get on top of the light. The darkness is at the footstool of the light. Light and blood have a predominant place in the currency of Heaven. Lucifer lost his place in glory. He went from being a covering cherubim in the throne room of God to being cast down to a planet of darkness and chaos where he is known as the prince of darkness. So we can see that the currency of light and blood have dominion over the fallen one.

BLOOD HAS A VOICE

It's so exciting when science catches up to biblical truth. Science has discovered that when light comes in contact with red blood cells, it releases sound waves. The sound waves seem to produce high frequency sound

waves that are above hearing by the human ear, but not out of the spiritual ear. Just think, the blood releases a sound that no doubt travels faster than the speed of sound, probably at the speed of light. When God asked Cain where his brother Abel was, Cain flippantly said, "I don't know, am I my brother's keeper?" God knew what had happened but wanted Cain to confess. Then the Lord said, *"What have you done? Listen! Your brother's blood cries out to me from the ground"* (see Genesis 4:9-10 NIV). The life in Abel that was given through the life of God to Adam had a voice.

If the blood of Adam, which had been corrupted through disobedience, had a voice, how much more the incorruptible blood of Jesus reverberates throughout the heavens. When light and glory connect with the blood of Jesus, there is movement in the heavens and darkness is lowered before us. John 1:3 (NKJV) makes an incredible statement: *"All things were made through Him, and without Him nothing was made that was made."* This is so powerful when we start linking these elements together. Nothing was created without Jesus the Son and the Holy Spirit. God would speak, and the Holy Spirit manifested the word of God. The Lamb of God was present at creation. Revelation 13:8 describes the Lamb of God as being slain from the foundation of the world, meaning it was predetermined what the Son of God would do.

The same power and glory that was present at creation is now resident in every believer. Know that the voice spoken at creation speaks through the blood of Jesus through us today. Hebrews 1:2-3 (KJV):

> *Hath in these last days spoken unto us by his Son, whom he hath appointed heir of all things, by whom also he made the worlds; who being the brightness of his glory, and the express image of his person, and upholding all things by the word of his*

> *power, when he had by himself purged our sins, sat down on the right hand of the Majesty on high.*

Since we are in the last days (beginning at resurrection), we are being communicated to by the Son and Holy Spirit.

A very interesting word in this verse will change how you to connect to the blood of Jesus. Jesus is the express image or the person of the Father. The word *person* is actually a compound word. *Per* meaning to pass through and *son* meaning sound or sonic. So, we could say Jesus is who the sound of the Father passes through. Since Christ dwells in us, we can also say we are ones the sound of the blood passes through.

Matthew 27:46-53 records the final hours of Jesus suspended on the cross between Heaven and earth. As His blood hit the ground and Jesus yielded up His spirit as the final sacrifice, the veil of the Temple was torn from top to bottom. Matthew 27:51 (NKJV) says, *"Then, behold, the veil of the temple was torn in two from top to bottom; and the earth quaked, and the rocks were split."* There was an earthquake. At that time His voice shook the earth, but now He has promised in Hebrews 12:26 (NKJV), *"Yet once more I will shake not only the earth, but also heaven."*

And the voice of God was also heard on Mountain of Sinai, and it shook the earth around them. The voice of the blood of Jesus not only shook the earth but now shook the heavens, meaning the second and third heavens. The second heaven is where the fallen angels have their domain in darkness. Then His blood was placed on the Mercy Seat to settle the redemption debt of sin for all time.

What Adam had lost in the Garden of Eden, Jesus restored and severed the headship of the devil over the seed of Adam. The bloodline of Cain was cleansed, and we were brought close to God by the blood of Jesus. *"But now in Christ Jesus you who once were far off have been brought*

near by the blood of Christ" (Ephesians 2:13 NKJV). You and I are now close to God through His blood, which means that now we too have a voice in the heavens.

As an anointed cherub, or light bearer, until iniquity was found in him, Lucifer was referred to as the morning star (Ezekiel 28:14). Jesus the Son was called the Bright and Morning Star. Lucifer understood the power of light and glory, but he lost his beauty and fell into darkness. He knows the power and authority of those who choose to live and serve in light. Psalm 119:130 (NKJV) says, *"The entrance of Your words gives light."* The words of God activate the light or revelation of His blood. When the light and blood come together, deliverance is released.

THE BLOOD SPEAKS

Hebrews 12:24 (NKJV) says, *"To Jesus the mediator of a new covenant, and to the sprinkled blood that speaks a better word than the blood of Abel."* The word *mediator* stands out as the emphasis of this passage. The Greek word for *mediator* is *mesos,* simply meaning to be in the middle. It is obvious that Jesus put Himself in the middle between God and man. But even more so, Jesus has put Himself between us and our enemy the devil. His blood comes between the slavery of sin and the deliverance we all need. We can easily see this advocacy of His blood in the Exodus story when He called His people out of Egyptian slavery. Exodus 12 shows us not only the symbolism of the blood of the lamb chosen for each house, but we can recognize the power of the currency of the blood of the Lamb of God. The Lord spoke to Moses:

This month shall be your beginning of months; it shall be the first month of the year to you. Speak to all the congregation of Israel, saying: "On the tenth of this month every man shall take for himself a lamb, according to the house of his father, a lamb for a household. And if the household is too small for the lamb, let him and his neighbor next to his house take it according to the number of the persons; according to each man's need you shall make your count for the lamb. Your lamb shall be without blemish, a male of the first year. You may take it from the sheep or from the goats. Now you shall keep it until the fourteenth day of the same month. Then the whole assembly of the congregation of Israel shall kill it at twilight. And they shall take some of the blood and put it on the two doorposts and on the lintel of the houses where they eat it" (Exodus 12:2-7 NKJV).

Passover was a reset of their calendar, but it would be a reset of life as well—from a life of slavery to a lifetime of freedom in relationship with the God they had yet to know. Passover represented deliverance and transformation. Understanding the power of the blood covenant gives us access into the throne room of God. The people were instructed to choose a lamb that was to be inspected free of blemishes. Exodus 12:13 (NKJV) says, *"Now the blood shall be a sign for you on the houses where you are. And when I see the blood, I will pass over you; and the plague shall not be on you to destroy you when I strike the land of Egypt."* Most of us probably read this verse and picture God as flying through the land of Egypt looking for the marked houses that would be spared from destruction, and destroying the firstborn in the houses not marked by blood.

The word *Passover* is translated *Pesach*, which means to cover or huddle over. This means when God sees the blood on the doorframe of the

house, He will come and cover or overshadow that house. Though God allowed the death angel to go through and bring judgment, God is not doing the killing. Revelation 9:1-4 (KJV) reveals:

> *And the fifth angel sounded, and I saw a star fall from heaven unto the earth: and to him was given the key to the bottomless pit. And he opened the bottomless pit; and there arose a smoke out of the pit, as the smoke of a great furnace; and the sun and the air were darkened by reason of the smoke of the pit. And there came out of the smoke locusts upon the earth: and unto them was given power, as the scorpions of the earth have power. And it was commanded them that they should not hurt the grass of the earth, neither any green thing, neither any tree; but only those men who have not the seal of God in their foreheads.*

I suggest to you this fallen angel with a key to the bottomless pit is the spirit of Abaddon, the destroyer that passes through the land, while the Lord is covering the houses of those under the blood covenant. God is attracted to the blood of His Son, and the destroyer has no dominion where the blood is applied. The blood of Abel brought attention into the heavens and Abel's blood was of the contaminated bloodline, so how much more now the blood of Jesus without the contamination of the first Adam, pure and undefiled will bring about the reaction of the heavenly host through Jesus Christ the second Adam. The apostle Paul wrote to the Corinthians: *"So it is written: 'The first man Adam became a living being'; the last Adam, a life-giving spirit. The spiritual did not come first, but the natural, and after that the spiritual"* (1 Corinthians 15:45-46 NIV).

Luke 1:30-37 (NKJV) is one the most exciting revelations in the New Testament. The angel Gabriel comes to a young virgin named Mary and announces she will have a son. She immediately voices her confusion by saying she has not been with a man. Gabriel explains this birth will not come from a human bloodline, but would come through the overshadowing or inseminating of the glory of God. Verse 37 finishes off this exchange by saying *"with God nothing will be impossible."*

The interesting point to this is the word *nothing*. Strangely enough it is translated in the Greek as *rhema*. *Rhema* is the Word of God, but more deeply it is the Word that has inside of itself the ability to do or create everything it was sent to do. Obviously, every seed has its own specific DNA inside of what it will produce. Corn won't produce wheat, etc. Seed is also translated as *sperma*. When the Holy Spirit overshadowed Mary, the bloodline was the DNA of Jehovah the seed from another world, Heaven itself, and it can only reproduce a heavenly bloodline. The Blood of Jesus speaks better things and will produce better results than Adam. Adam gave away his authority in the Garden of Eden.

In the Garden of Gethsemane, Jesus reclaimed the bloodline that would give us access into the Kingdom of God. This currency that is upon us has no response from darkness. There is nothing that the devil can say against the currency of Heaven, which is the most precious and valuable gift ever given to us. Not only does it cleanse us from sin, it is a weapon that has already severed the headship of the devil. This blood of the Lamb has been deposited into your account for you to use in your defense and as offensive weaponry.

First Peter 1:18-19 (NKJV) says that *"you were not redeemed with corruptible things, like silver or gold, from your aimless conduct received by tradition from your fathers, but with the precious blood of Christ, as of a lamb without blemish and without spot."* The concept of redeemed or redemption means more than restoring to the last time we were happy.

Redemption means to go back to the point of God's original plan before the fall of humankind. It takes the currency of the blood of Jesus to see that accomplished. When we understand how to use the currency of Heaven, we will pray and declare His Word with redemption in mind. Currency prayer is not to fix a temporary problem but to fulfill the mandate that God agreed to with His Son (for more understanding, read my book, *The Secret Power of Covenant*).

"Let the redeemed of the Lord say so, whom he hath redeemed from the hand of the enemy; and gathered them out of the lands, from the east, and from the west, from the north, and from the south" (Psalm 107:2-3 NKJV). The blood of Jesus through His redemption has a story to tell that is filled with His power and might.

When the revelation of His blood currency takes hold of your life, your conversation changes from shame and defeat to one of the power of His resurrection. The blood of the Lamb has a voice, and the voice is now in you—but the language is not yours, it is throne room language. *"I fell at his feet to worship him. And he said unto me, See thou do it not: I am thy fellowservant, and of thy brethren that have the testimony of Jesus: worship God: for the testimony of Jesus is the spirit of prophecy"* (Revelation 19:10 KJV). The blood of Jesus prophesies to the things that have not yet been redeemed or brought back into God's domain.

We carry the DNA of the blood that prophesies of the story of resurrection so we can, through His blood, see and proclaim that all our family will come to know the lordship of Christ. Forever truth is revealed in the Word of God. The devil will attempt to contrast and use counterfeit currency in his kingdom of darkness. The currency the devil and those who operate in darkness will try to use the currency of fear, doubt and unbelief. This thought begs the question as to what language or currency are you using?

Just like the currency of Heaven uses the Word of God and activates the response of angels, is it possible that our currency of anger and complaining could be releasing the domain of the fallen angels? The power of agreement not only works in the Kingdom of God, it also works in the underworld of darkness. Whatever or whoever we are partnering with, we bring into our world or home their agenda and power. *"But I say, that the things which the Gentiles sacrifice, they sacrifice to devils, and not to God: and I would not that ye should have fellowship with devils"* (1 Corinthians 10:20 KJV). Paul is obviously referring to the Lord's Table and using meat offered to idols; however, he connects to the idea that we can attract demons by our interaction with things they identify with. In this case our language of defeat and bitterness is an identifier to dark forces that see that as a legal right to enter your domain.

Regarding our topic context, the Bible mentions three seats:

1. Psalm 1:1 (NIV) says, *"Blessed is the one who does not walk in step with the wicked or stand in the way that sinners take or sit in the company of mockers."*

2. Ephesians 2:6 (NIV) says, *"God raised us up with Christ and seated us with him in the heavenly realms in Christ Jesus."*

3. The third seat mentioned is in Revelation 2:13 (NIV) the angel of the church of Pergamos writes saying *"I know where you live—where Satan has his throne."*

All three of these seats have their own identifying language or payback system. The easy question to ask here is: To which seats do you have access? Each seat or throne represents a type of authority and agreement.

Paul tells us in 2 Corinthians 6:14 (NKJV): *"Do not be unequally yoked together with unbelievers. For what fellowship has righteousness with lawlessness? And what communion has light with darkness?"* Paul is asking the same question. Fellowship doesn't necessarily mean you like the person or thing you are yoked to, but it reveals language we are attracting.

RIGHT FIGHTERS

Let me explain how this works. Some years ago I was counseling a couple who had made many attempts with other counselors to resolve their issues. Before we started, I told them that I was going to pray and get to the root habitation of their problems since talking about symptoms only served to stir up the anger between them.

Suddenly what popped out of my mouth was surprising to them, and me. I said, "It's time you break up with the devil and divorce his headship." Observing the look on their faces, I knew I had some explaining to do and I was eager to hear it myself. I slowly took them back to their conversations with one another and each felt their argument was to prove they were right; basically, they were "right fighters." Their words sunk deep into each other and after a while they felt even anointed in their passion to hurt or prove their seated position was correct.

They had been using the currency of cursing and the demons loved helping them get deeper into soul debt. I could see their demeanor begin to change as they were catching the perfumery of the Holy Spirit. They quickly repented to each other and then we declared a divorce decree over the yoke of the devil. You could say they changed seats and moved into a higher currency of the heavenly where righteousness was the only side to stand on.

Now instead of being "Right Fighters," they are fighting every day for the righteousness in Christ Jesus. The change of seat revealed a change of perspective. Proverbs 18:21 (NKJV) tells us, *"Death and life are in the power of the tongue, and those who love it will eat its fruit."* There are two kingdoms—one of life and one of death—and you access the kingdoms through your choice of language. John 1:3 says, *"All things were made through Him, and without Him nothing was made that was made."* Since *"Him"* is referring to Jesus the Word of God in flesh, we can easily see that we are making things that are created through the life of the Word of God—or death through cursing and unbelief.

Jesus quoting from Deuteronomy 8:3 says, *"Man shall not live by bread alone, but by every word that proceeds from the mouth of God."* The true life of living in the Spirit of Christ is to live by the word or currency that proceeds from the mouth of God.

3

The Currency
OF FAITH

S AM came to me, as he was facing a huge felony case against him. I had never met him before, but a neighbor recommended that he make an appointment with me. The felony charge was horrendous and disgusting to the natural thinking. I was doing my best to respond as a counselor and not add any of my own objections. It was obvious Sam was not a believer. When I questioned him about his relationship with Jesus, he asserted that he was probably more on the line of an agnostic. I asked him what he meant by "agnostic." I could tell he was doing his best to be sincere. He described it as, "Well, I know there must be some kind of entity out there that brought about what I see around me."

I could see that he didn't have a clue as to the severity of the charges he was facing. He grew up in a home where abuse and molestation were more of a rite of passage than anything else. The god of this world had literally blinded his eyes from any reasonable sense of morality or normalcy.

Quietly under my breath I asked for the leadership of the Holy Spirit to show me what to say. As soon as I asked for help from the Holy Spirit,

I was prompted to ask Sam what kind of work he did. He responded that he was a commercial electrician and presently working on a large project at a school. I then saw a picture with my spiritual eyes of him working with large voltage, such as 440 3-phase. I asked him what would possess a sane man to put his hand inside a panel of such powerful voltage. He quickly responded by saying, "Because I know the breaker to that circuit is off." I said him, "So, you are willing to stake your whole life on a screw and a spring on that breaker to hold?"

Sam responded with a statement that would change his life forever. He said, "I have to believe that the breaker is working." As soon as he said that his eyes widened as big as golf balls. "You mean that all I need to do is believe in Jesus?" I answered yes and led him through a simple prayer. Seconds later as if someone had taken a blindfold from his eyes, he began to cry saying, "My God, what have I done." Minutes before he had no sense as to why he was charged for anything.

Not only did the Holy Spirt reveal Jesus to Sam, He brought a spirit of repentance to him as well. Sam went on to serve many years in the penitentiary for his crime. We kept in touch by letters from time to time. Sam ended up leading many of his inmate friends to Jesus as he worked with the chaplain. He also completed a number of Bible school degrees. While working in the prison hospital and hospice, Sam was able to present Jesus to those who had never received Christ before.

I saw firsthand that day how powerful faith was in activating righteousness in Sam's life. The Holy Spirit changed the trajectory of his life that was heading for destruction. Faith was the activation that opened the door to many wonderful things for Sam that would have otherwise been closed to him, and he would have never even known the glory that lied before him.

FAITH, YOUR ACCOUNT ACTIVATOR

Faith is both a noun and a verb. That may sound strange to think of it as a grammatical statement, but it's true. If I only think of faith as a noun, then it simply describes a static position. For instance, I can say my faith is Christian, distinguishing me from other types of religions or faiths. When faith activates what is deposited in Heaven, then faith becomes a verb that requires action on my part. James 2:17-19 (NKJV) says, *"Thus also faith by itself, if it does not have works, is dead. But someone will say, 'You have faith, and I have works.' Show me your faith without your works, and I will show you my faith by my works. You believe that there is one God. You do well. Even the demons believe and tremble!"*

Notice how James makes the distinction between faith as a noun and faith as a verb. Faith by itself is a stated noun, but when faith starts to move in what we are called to do, then faith starts activating the power of the Word of God. James makes a stunning statement that even the demons believe and tremble. What this means is that believing is simply "possibility thinking" or "I believe it's possible." If all I have is a belief system without a faith system, then I am only at a demonic level.

When we act on what we believe, it is transformative—it turns a stagnant pool of water into a flowing river moving things along with its flow. There is life in a river of active faith, but in motionless pools things die from religious pollution. When religion is solely a faith statement, it is a dead pool of beliefs. Faith without works is dead—and the antithesis of this is faith working toward the Word bringing life. Simply put, faith turns on the power to change the status from death to life and weakness to strength. For example, the reason some businesses install motion detectors in their light switches is because people don't remember to

turn off the lights. The point being, there must be movement to turn on the power to the lights.

Faith without movement is a noun, not a verb that takes action and turns on the switch. I am convinced a lot of unanswered prayers have gone silent due to no movement toward what they are believing for.

When I was 19 years old my pastor and those around me recognized that I was called to preach, and there was even prophecy spoken over me confirming as such. I was issued a license to minister. The only thing was, I had never officially shared with anyone or any group a message or sermon. Although I felt accepted among my peers as having joined their ranks, I had the noun kind of faith; it was a statement that I could preach yet without works. The time came when I was called upon to ratify my calling of faith. I could say it was time "to fish or cut bait," as my ministry could not stay in the noun form. The noun form of my faith was safe, and I had not yet made any mistakes. Yet, there was no power in my noun type of faith only an outward appearance of faith.

Well it was bound to happen, it was time to share my first message, or sermon, and there was no way I could go backward after claiming faith. After spending hours in study, I asked the Holy Spirit to enable me not to fail. I guess failure meant stage fright and being tongue-tied.

The first few minutes of speaking seemed to me like I was shooting in the dark. Then I noticed a sense of boldness kick in—and to my surprise I was saying things that I had not written into my notes. Eventually I forgot about my notes entirely. I realized that my faith left the noun position and moved into the working groove that made all the difference in the world. No longer would I say I had faith, now I could say I move in faith. Things happen when we move in faith, then faith starts to move us.

Faith is proportionate to the willingness to trust the Holy Spirit and obey the prompting of His Word. Romans 12:3 (NIV) says, *"For by the grace given me I say to every one of you: Do not think of yourself more highly than you ought, but rather think of yourself with sober judgment, in accordance with the* [measure of] *faith God has distributed to each of you."* Paul is reminding us that we all have been given a measure (*metron*) of faith. Simply put, the beginning of a seed has been given to all of us. However, it is up to us if the measure of faith remains solely a noun or moves into a life-transforming verb. Faith is much more than a mantra of repetitive sayings; faith must leave the barn and get to plowing the field where you will sow to bring it to its potential.

When Moses brought the Hebrews out from Egypt, they were facing the Red Sea with the Egyptian army pursuing from behind. The picture most of us have of the scene is the Hebrews' panic, even some blaming Moses for bring them to die in the desert. God tells Moses to stretch his rod over the sea. The sea began to part, and the miracle of their deliverance was realized. The same sea that gave them passage was the same sea that brought destruction to their enemies.

The second time the Hebrews were at a water crossing was at the Jordan River (Joshua 3:8). This time they were required to have the priests who were carrying the Ark of the Covenant to first step into the Jordan. Their first crossing at the Red Sea was one person responding with a rod; this time it was a team having to step into the water first before they saw the miracle of water parting.

The level of faith for something to happen many times calls for action on our part. It is the same for us today; the increase of faith calls for an increase of trust and acting on what we sense the Holy Spirit leading us to do. Faith is not a leap into the dark; it's a walk in the light. Faith is like radar that enables us to see through the fog so we can keep moving forward. Faith does not work well when we stop to consult our feelings,

which allows fear to have a say in the direction we are heading. Consult the Holy Spirit—He knows the way.

> *I have been crucified with Christ and I no longer live, but Christ lives in me. The life I now live in the body, I live by faith in the Son of God, who loved me and gave himself for me* (Galatians 2:20 NIV).

The main point I want to make here is the faith of the Son of God. When we allow the Holy Spirit to crucify the natural thinking of the soul that is in opposition to God, then the faith of the Son engages our spirit and leads us into the purpose for which we were designed to do (Romans 8:7). Your potential is locked up inside you, and it takes the Holy Spirit to unlock the soul for your potential to run freely and be a co-heir and partner in His creation.

MISDIRECTED FAITH

While Jesus was among the people, a man called out to Jesus to have mercy upon his son who was an epileptic and would often fall into the fire or water. The father went on to explain that he brought his son to the disciples, but they were not able to cure him. Jesus instructed the man to bring the boy to Him and He rebuked the demon, and the child was cured. Jesus said openly this was a *"faithless and perverse generation"* (Matthew 17:17 NKJV).

> *And Jesus rebuked the demon, and it came out of him; and the child was cured from that very hour. Then the disciples came*

to Jesus privately and said, "Why could we not cast it out?" So Jesus said to them, "Because of your unbelief; for assuredly, I say to you, if you have faith as a mustard seed, you will say to this mountain, 'Move from here to there,' and it will move; and nothing will be impossible for you. However, this kind does not go out except by prayer and fasting" (Matthew 17:18-21 NKJV).

Jesus does acknowledge that the demon was of a higher rank. Possibly the disciples at that time had an empty account or their level of faith had yet to be developed. Jesus plainly says they couldn't cast out the demon because of their unbelief. They had seen Jesus numerous times cast out demons. This time He told them fasting and prayer would be effective. The purpose of fasting is to bring the carnal flesh under subjection of the spirit. It is possible for us to know the methodology of how to cast out demons or heal the sick, but we must always be aware of the One who deserves our focus—Jesus, the One in whom our faith is centered. What I mean by misdirected faith is that faith can be focused on the problem rather than on the Person of our faith.

Hebrews 12:2 says Jesus is *"the Author and Finisher of our faith."* When faith emulates the Originator of faith, then we are living in the faith of the Son of God. The demonic realm recognizes that faith flows from Him. In reading the Genesis account of the creation of man, the word *likeness* stands out. It originally was intended to mean in the liking of God or being like Him in thought and action. Putting faith in the teaching of faith is not faith. Faith is an intimate relationship to the One who gives faith; and the more we respond in the likeness of God, the greater faith has a place in us. We cannot separate faith from the intimate relationship we have with the Originator of faith.

WITHOUT FAITH THE DOOR IS CLOSED

John 10 clearly teaches us that Jesus is the door into the sheepfold, and those who are truly His sheep hear His voice. Since Jesus is the door to the Father, He certainly is the door into our heavenly currency account. Hebrews 11:6 (NKJV) says, *"But without faith it is impossible to please Him, for he who comes to God must believe that He is, and that He is a rewarder of those who diligently seek Him."* The first step in finding favor and accessing the currency of Heaven is to please the Lord. It is interesting to note that the word in the Greek for *pleasing* is akin to *yes*. Then, we could say it's impossible to say "Yes" to God without faith. Operating in faith is like saying yes to God.

> *By faith Abel offered to God a more excellent sacrifice than Cain, through which he obtained witness that he was righteous, God testifying of his gifts; and through it he being dead still speaks* (Hebrews 11:4 NKJV).

Abel's name is in the faith hall of fame because he offered the sacrifice to God that said yes, by faith. His faith still has a voice to us thousands of years later. You can see that the blood of Jesus has a voice and faith has a voice. Though you may not be speaking right now, your faith has a sound that the kingdom of darkness hears. Your faith continues to build an account in Heaven that you can draw from. Your faith is always speaking and always leading into right thinking and right doing.

Abel's brother Cain offered a sacrifice, but it was not offered in faith. He offered in response to God what he wanted to give, but it was not a sacrifice that pleased or said yes to God. Faith is more than a response, it the correct response that God wants.

Misguided faith misses the target when it is not the yes God wants to hear. James 4:3 (KJV) says, *"Ye ask, and receive not, because ye ask amiss, that ye may consume it upon your lusts."* True faith doesn't miss the target, it first pleases the Lord. *"When a man's ways please the Lord, He makes even his enemies to be at peace with him"* (Proverbs 16:7 NKJV). The application is when we say yes, we are acting in faith which causes our enemies to be at peace with us. I have a personal picture of this verse where my enemy is like a troll that won't let me cross the bridge without paying a toll. But when our ways please the Lord, the troll must step aside and let me pass. Though the devil doesn't like stepping aside and giving up his territory, faith demands it because we are drawing on the authority that has been deposited on our behalf.

UNVEILING FAITH

Faith that is based on personal encounters with the Lord is always unveiling to reveal what the Lord has in store for you. Whatever has been stored up for you is unlocked and brought out into the open through active, advancing faith. Faith doesn't retreat, it always moves toward the evidence through the Word of God that you have the right, plus the authority, to expand your boundaries.

> *For the word of God is living and powerful, and sharper than any two-edged sword, piercing even to the division of soul and spirit, and of joints and marrow, and is a discerner of the thoughts and intents of the heart* (Hebrews 4:12 NKJV).

The important thing to know is the Word of God is active, never passive, and always present to advance the purpose for which it was sent. When the active, creative word is joined with faith, it unlocks the mysteries of the Kingdom of God. The word interacts with our spirit from an eternal perspective. Ecclesiastes 3:11 (NIV) says, God *"has also set eternity in the human heart."* This tells us we are more eternal than temporal. When the word is active in our innermost being, it will distinguish between what is happening in our soul from our spirit. The active word will excite our spirit; and when we allow faith to connect with that prompting, something wonderful will take place. Paul makes it clear that the word without the spirit is a dead or deadly letter like what the Pharisees used to control the people of their day with—fear of judgment at the slightest infraction of the law.

Faith unveils the will and potential, while a legal form of religion seeks to lock up the power of God. Faith reveals the real you that has been awakened by the Spirit to do incredible exploits. Second Corinthians 4:16 (NIV) reminds us, *"Therefore we do not lose heart. Though outwardly we are wasting away, yet inwardly we being renewed day by day."* We were created with the inner self being refreshed and redeemed to fulfill the original purpose before the fall of Adam, which was to rule and reign with the Lord on earth. Faith stirs the new inner self to come forward beyond the carnal, soulish old self. The devil hates us because he sees something that most people don't see. God placed something in the redeemed that He wants to keep us blind toward.

According to Isaiah 14 we can gain some insight into the purpose of lucifer, the angel/cherubim who was to oversee the worship and glory around the throne of God. He was created for sound with various pipes and strings—a sort of surround sound. He was once the morning star; however, the Son of God is called the Bright and Morning Star.

Lucifer was cast out of Heaven into a planet of darkness; his name was changed to adversary and the prince of darkness. He knows how powerful the glory of God is. In the New Covenant we have become a new type of the Ark of Covenant. The glory that was once was confined to a box has now been transferred by grace through faith into us. When the devil sees you, he is not looking at the outside, he sees the glory of God that has been placed inside you. You are more than a bag of bones; you are a carrier of the glory of the begotten Son.

Colossians 1:26-27 (NKJV) tells us, *"the mystery which has been hidden from ages and from generations, but now has been revealed to His saints. To them God willed to make known what the riches of the glory of this mystery among the Gentiles are: which is Christ in you, the hope of glory."* The glory that was hidden in earthen human vessels is being unveiled with every increase of your faith.

When the word is stirring inside you and you respond in faith, the glory of the Lord is unveiled and miracles take place. When your faith says yes to God, there is an agreement between Heaven and earth that causes a manifestation of the unseen becoming the seen. *"For it is the God who commanded light to shine out of darkness, who has shone in our hearts to give the light of the knowledge of the glory of God in the face of Jesus Christ"* (2 Corinthians 4:6-7 NKJV). But we have this treasure in earthen vessels, that the excellence of the power may be of God and not of us.

SURPRISED BY THE SPIRIT

Many years ago, I ventured to take a group of teenagers to Costa Rica for a week of ministry. The itinerary called for us to minister in a different

church each evening for a week. Most of the group were seventeen- and eighteen-year-olds. None of them had never been outside of the United States. Looking back, I ask myself, *What was I thinking?* But there was a surprise ending for all of us. The format was for the team to share their testimonies and a short exhortation, then at the end of my message they would help pray over those responding to the altar call. At the beginning of the week there was the normal inattentive minds and they looked more like tourists than serious ministers.

As the week progressed, though, the ministry part of the trip became more intense. The last night we were in the small town of Cartago. The demonic spirits were being tormented by us being there. At the end of the message, numerous people responded to the invitation of freedom from demonic torment. The young ministry team's faith was continually growing each evening of ministry. I could tell they were ready and anxious to begin. It was obvious there was something different about this place and this evening. Their discernment had increased enough that they realized it would take more than simply praying for them. They soon would see that the time had come for their prayers to be empowered with authority from the One they had been praying to using the name of Jesus.

The young ministers laid hands on a good number of people showing signs of demonic activity. One by one the demons left, some thrashing around on the ground, others screaming out. I was proud of our team because it didn't seem to intimidate or dissuade them from their mission of bringing freedom.

Soon those who were once bound began to rejoice in their new transformation. Priceless to me were the looks on the faces of the young troop who were astonished to see the power of God flowing through them and driving out darkness. Their faith had outgrown any doubt they might have had before. One young man stared at his hands saying, "I didn't

know I had it in me." Faith had plugged them into the unseen realm where they would never forget or question the power of God. *"So we fix our eyes not on what is seen, but on what is unseen, since what is seen is temporary, but what is unseen is eternal"* (2 Corinthians 4:18 NIV). Faith has been given to us to see what is unseen and do what is not doable in our ability. Faith is looking for channels to flow through to activate the Word of God.

Remember, faith is substance that stirs hope, and hope is not wishful thinking, it anchors the soul to the Word of God. Second, faith is evidence that is inside our inner self, our spirit. Our spirit has the evidence, but if the soul has no anchor that solidly connects to an intimate interaction continually with Jesus, the soul is tossed around by the wind and waves of this life like a ship driven by whatever is happening around it. The soul can be the lid, or it can cooperate with our spirit to see the manifestation of God's awesome power to bring dead things to life or to move the unmovable. Nothing is impossible for those who first believe—then act in faith.

WHOLLY INTEGRATED

"And the very God of peace sanctify you wholly; and I pray God your whole spirit and soul and body be preserved blameless unto the coming of our Lord Jesus Christ" (1 Thessalonians 5:23 KJV). In this verse, the apostle Paul is giving some very valuable instructions to believers. For context, he is telling the people in the previous verses to give thanks in all things, don't quench the spirit, and do not despise prophecy. Paul goes on to declare about wholeness. The wholeness he is referring to concerns the integration of all parts of our being. We consist of a body, a soul, and

a spirit. When these three work independently of one another and independently of the Holy Spirit, we are operating on less than the optimum of how God designed us. It would be like an eight-cylinder truck designed to haul or pull heavy loads with only four cylinders firing.

We were created to be a synchronized creation where our spirit is to be dominant, our soul (mind, will, emotions, intellect) is to submit, and our bodies respond to what is happening to the other two parts. Many times, the body is a reflection of what is happening in our emotions, and the emotions reflect the peace and security we have in our spirit. Paul's prayer is that our whole three-part being will be sanctified, meaning cleansed, for exclusive use by the Lord. Also, I find interesting the language Paul uses in this passage by including in his prayer that we would be preserved blameless unto the coming of the Lord Jesus Christ. The Greek word for *blameless* here is *amemptos,* which means "to prove that there is no mixture." In one sense the soul is to prove that it is free from all the allures that the god of this world will cast before it.

When our spirit is in charge and our minds are submitted to the working of the Holy Spirit through our spirit, traps are revealed and we are less likely to be deceived into succumbing to the wiles of the enemy. In the beginning of creation when God created Adam and Eve, they were dominated and led by their spirit—the part that set them apart from all other creatures and creation. The spirit of Adam and Eve came directly from the breath of God when He breathed into Adam and Adam became a living being. The original text says that Adam became a "speaking spirit." Adam had the very essence of God who is Spirit. This spirit dimension in Adam gave him the ability to communicate with God through spirit to Spirit. Adam didn't have to guess at what God's intentions or will was, Adam just knew in his spirit.

When Adam stepped across the line from when they were wholly belonging to God to disobeying and eating of the Tree of the Knowledge

of Good and Evil, everything about their relationship with God flipped. The glory of God that covered their naked bodies left, and for the first time they saw each other without the lens of glory. Immediately they became more dominant in their minds, and their spirits were now on the bottom rung of the ladder, so to speak. Now that their minds, or souls, were in charge, they hid themselves from the presence of God.

For the first time in creation, they ran from the presence of God.

Now that their souls were in charge, they started blaming each other. Adam blamed the woman God gave him, and the woman blamed the devil. We certainly can't disconnect our soul from the rest of our being, however. Paul reminds us in 1 Corinthians 2:16 (NKJV), *"For 'who has known the mind of the Lord that he may instruct Him?' But we have the mind of Christ."* The very thing that causes us to move from simply believing into activated faith is to train our minds to come into the image of the mind of Christ. We have the elements present in us from creation, we just need to allow the Holy Spirit to raise up the mind of Christ over our own mindsets.

THE TESTING OF FAITH

Faith mentioned in the Bible seems to get tested. For example, Jesus told Peter in Luke 22:28-32:

> *But you are those who have continued with Me in My trials. And I bestow upon you a kingdom, just as My Father bestowed one upon Me, that you may eat and drink at My table in My kingdom, and sit on thrones judging the twelve tribes of Israel." And the Lord said, "Simon, Simon! Indeed, Satan has*

> *asked for you, that he may sift you as wheat. But I have prayed*
> *for you, that your faith should not fail; and when you have*
> *returned to Me, strengthen your brethren.*

It's amazing to me that Jesus didn't offer any challenge to Peter or advice as to how he should handle what was coming. Peter failed when he was tested, which resulted in the three-time denial Jesus had forecasted. It was the testing of his faith that revealed to Peter himself where his heart was. I am sure Peter felt he was up for the challenge and had boasted he would stand with Jesus even unto death.

The testing of our faith is not for others to observe our courage, it is for the purpose of us knowing where we are regarding our level of faith. Peter did go on to do amazing things as one of the major apostles in the New Testament. The reason we need testing is not to show how weak we are but to identify how much we need the strength of the Holy Spirit to partner with us to do what He said we could if we only had faith. The faith we need is not our own self will and resolve, but in God. The King of faith comes when we realize He really is the Author and Finisher of our faith. Our faith really becomes the faith of the Son of God (Galatians 2:20).

Faith really has two parts to its success: the *hearing* of faith that we all begin with and cited in Romans 10:17 (NKJV), "*faith comes by hearing.*" And the second part is the *doing* of faith. Hearing without doing is not completed faith. If you were one of Jesus' early disciples hanging out with Peter and the other fishermen and heard Jesus say to the group, "Come follow Me and I will make you fishers of men," you may have thought, *That's really inspiring.* But the disciples heard Him and then went back to doing what they were doing before Jesus spoke. Peter heard, hearing from faith, but nothing changed for those who just listened. Again,

James says that faith without works is like a body without a spirit, which results in a dead body (see James 2:26).

Hebrews 12:27-28 (NKJV) says:

> *Now this, "Yet once more," indicates the removal of those things that are being shaken, as of things that are made, that the things which cannot be shaken may remain. Therefore, since we are receiving a kingdom which cannot be shaken, let us have grace, by which we may serve God acceptably with reverence and godly fear.*

No one really likes the idea of being tested, but one thing for sure is that a test is usually an indication you are coming to the end of something. When I was in school, I knew tests, at least the big ones, came at the end of a semester. When things are being shaken, it is for the purpose of removing anything that doesn't belong in the next phase of the building process.

Testing in the biblical sense is not necessarily punitive, but for graduation from one season or level to the next. Anything God tests is for the purpose of strengthening faith. Resistance builds muscle and faith, resistance causes one to increase in faith and resolve. Faith presses on through the resistance. James 1:2-4 (NKJV) says, *"My brethren, count it all joy when you fall into various trials, knowing that the testing of your faith produces patience. But let patience have its perfect work, that you may be perfect and complete, lacking nothing."* Patience in this context is important. The Greek word for patience is *hupomone*, which means "to remain under the covering." Putting it another way, we could say be happy when resistance comes your way and stay under the covering of

faith so that you may be complete, missing out on nothing. Think of it as a graduation ceremony when you remain in faith-advance mode.

When my faith was tested, I didn't realize at the time it was a test. I just knew there was only one direction for me to go, and that was pursue, overtake, and recover (which is actually the title of my last book). The Greek word for *testing* used in James 1:2 is *dokimion* which is translated as the process of proving to be genuine or containing, no mixture. First Peter 4:12 (NIV) says, *"Dear friends, do not be surprised at the fiery ordeal that has come on you to test you, as though something strange were happening to you."* This verse equates fire to the issue of testing. The idea is when trying to bring gold to its purest form and separate it from all other non-gold materials, the raw material is heated to the point that the impurities would float to the surface and then would be skimmed off. The fiery test you may be going through at the time is not pleasurable, but just know your refined faith is being accounted to you as pure faith that has been refined and gives you greater authority.

Remember, faith advances and fear retreats. Faith looks forward to what can be, and fear looks back and wonders what could have been. James goes on to say in Chapter 1 that a double-minded person is not able to receive anything from the Lord and is unstable in all his ways. *Double-minded* means two souls conflicting in one person. Faith comes out of your spirit, not from the soul. So, standing under what the Word of God and the prompting of the Holy Spirit is saying to you will strengthen your faith with patience.

INCREASE OUR FAITH

Jesus' disciples had asked for their faith to be increased. There must have been something that clued them that they needed more than what they had. In response to their request, Jesus poses a parable to them to explain what increased faith looks like:

> *And which of you, having a servant plowing or tending sheep, will say to him when he has come in from the field, "Come at once and sit down to eat"? But will he not rather say to him, "Prepare something for my supper, and gird yourself and serve me till I have eaten and drunk, and afterward you will eat and drink"? Does he thank that servant because he did the things that were commanded him? I think not. So likewise, when you have done all those things which you are commanded, say, "We are unprofitable servants. We have done what was our duty to do"* (Luke 17:7-10 NKJV).

The lesson for the disciples was that faith increases when you go beyond the minimal, doing more than just what is expected.

We have the faith given to us to believe unto salvation, then we move on to increased faith through hearing the word of God, then great faith grows when we face an impossibility and continue to press through without doubting. Unusual faith is in the realm of the gift of faith—it is supernatural to accomplish something outside the realm of explanation.

Let me go back again for just a moment to increased faith. Romans 10:17 (NKJV) says, *"So then faith comes by hearing, and hearing by the word of God."* The instruction here is to hear the word of God, and we

develop hearing through the Word of God. This means much more than listening to the Word.

Listening and hearing in Scripture are two entirely different things. The word for *faith* is *pistis,* which means to believe to the point of confidence that is convincing and trust is unconditional. Paul is conveying the message to hear the word of God with such trust and confidence to the point it moves us to act upon what we heard. Increasing faith is not static based only on what you have heard—faith increases by what you are hearing and responding to what you are hearing.

In summation, faith is the activator to our account in Heaven and releases what is deposited for us to carry out our mission here on earth. The greater the faith, the greater the release of the power and authority given to us. Faith will not return void; it will accomplish what it was sent to do.

4

The Currency
OF JOY

J OY is a very important currency that is easily misunderstood. For most of us, we think of joy as being a positive emotion that makes us feel good and causes us to exhibit our best expectations for the day. The reason Heaven sees it as a currency or value is because it is not natural—joy is supernatural. What we usually think of as joy is probably happiness. Happiness is based on what is happening. If things are going favorable for us, we feel happy. Happiness and joy both make us feel emotional; however, joy comes from the Spirit of God, while happiness is derived from our soul. Joy lives and stirs our spirit while happiness exists in our soul or mind, will and intellect. Happiness can change in a moment when we are offended or our feelings are assaulted.

Happiness is very fickle and is like riding a roller coaster with highs and lows. Joy is always present with us although we are not always aware of it. Joy is always present with the Holy Spirit. The very nature of the Spirit of Christ is joy.

> *Your throne, O God will last for ever and ever, and a scep-*
> *ter of justice will be the scepter of your kingdom. You love*

> *righteousness and hate wickedness; therefore God, your God, has set you above your companions by anointing you with the oil of joy* (Psalm 45:6-7 NIV).

These verses are describing the Messiah who was being seen through the psalmist. The context is the rule and throne of Messiah. A scepter is a token of His dominion and authority, and the anointing placed upon Him is speaking of empowerment, which is the anointing of joy. This is only one reason I see joy as a currency seen by the throne of God as valuable. Certainly the psalmist is not referring to an emotion regarding the anointing upon the Messiah. Isaiah 10:27 (NKJV) tells us, *"It shall come to pass in that day that his burden will be taken away from your shoulder, and his yoke from your neck, and the yoke will be destroyed because of the anointing oil."*

The anointing oil in the Bible is significant due to the fact it was used primarily by kings and priests to place value upon or to separate from the common to something sacred or kingly. The yoke in Isaiah 10:27 represents the cruelty that the Assyrians inflicted on the Israelites. The yoke represents enslavement and control. A yoke ties something or some person to something else. The prophet Isaiah is declaring the anointing was going to break the yoke of slavery from the neck of God's people.

In the New Testament, anointing takes on a more accessible use of the anointing oil. The Greek word commonly used for *anointing* is *charisma* or *charis*. The words *Christ* or *Christos* is similar to meaning the Anointed One. Jesus Christ is the Anointed One. The psalmist was declaring that the Anointed One would be anointed with the oil of joy. One of the attributes of Christ is the anointing of joy, not the anointing for happiness. Another popular meaning for *anointing* is "to smear or rub with oil." The original would say the fatness or oil would break the yoke.

We would say today that the anointing inside a believer would be so fat it would break apart the external yoke. First John 4:4 (NKJV) says, *"You are of God, little children, and have overcome them, because He who is in you is greater than he who is in the world."* The Anointed One and His anointing in your spirit will break or explode the outer enslavement of the enemy. Let God arise and let His enemies be scattered (Psalm 68:1). When joy bubbles up, your enemies will scatter because it's not temporary happiness but the divine nature of the Anointed One.

THE EXPLOSION OF JOY

In 1994 there was an amazing and unusual impartation of joy. I was invited to attend a meeting in Rockwall, Texas, by my sister. She was describing some of this anointing of joy. I was somewhat skeptical but also curious at the same time. My wife, Diane, really wanted to go more than me. It was a couple of hours' drive. Somehow, we were seated on the third row. The place was filled with what was estimated by some to be more than three thousand. The service was unconventional to say the least. To an outside observer, which I was for the time being, I could see they had no planned agenda except only to wait for the Holy Spirit to reveal the plan. The worship was intimate and focused totally on the Lord. I felt the tenderness of the Holy Spirit and would have been happy to leave with just that.

After some exhortation about yielding to the Holy Spirit, we were invited to come forward for laying on of hands by the host of the meeting, which at that time was Rodney Howard Brown, whom I had never heard of. I looked over at Diane and said, "Are you ready to go since we have a two-hour drive?" She quickly said, "I'm going down front," very

close to where we were. She passed in front of me not waiting to see what I was going to do. I thought to myself, *If don't follow her down there I will lose her in this crowd.* I no sooner stepped up beside her when hands were placed on my head and I heard the words, "Fill, fill more, Lord." I went backward and laid on the floor wondering what just happened. I didn't feel anything unusual so I thought, *Since Diane is lying beside me on the carpet, I'll just rest here for a little bit since we have that long drive home. I'll wait till she's ready then we will head out.* I'm not sure how long the minute lasted, but I could see she was rustling a bit, so I got up and helped her up.

As I started toward the door, I noticed a couple of elders from my church. I didn't know they were there until then; one seemed to be, in my estimation, a little bit inebriated. Since we were comfortable with the infilling of the Holy Spirit, it wasn't strange to me. But for those two elders, I did think it was certainly different for them.

As soon as I opened the door to step into the hallway that encircled the sanctuary, I felt as if I stepped into a deep pool of refreshing. With my back against the door, I slid down until I was sitting on the floor, blocking the door. Then I begin to laugh hilariously for no apparent reason at all. I looked up at people stepping over me as they made their way toward the doors leading to the parking lot. And there was Diane who was watching me with a very pleasant grin on her face as if to say, "See there, you *did* need to go down front."

It was good there were many other doors for people to use to exit, because I couldn't calculate how long I was in that strange position; something wonderful filled my entire being, body, soul, and spirit. This was the joy of the Lord, and I felt so close to my Lord; all the while, I could sense a cleansing going on from all the hurts and wounds I had acquired as a pastor. As I finally exited the building, I could see there were scores of others who were having similar experiences. The next

Sunday, I made sure that no one that knew what had happened just two evenings before. I did not want to cause a copycat reaction. Also, I thought it was just probably what I needed.

The next Sunday standing on the platform next to the elders as is our custom, worship again was very intimate with the Lord. Then suddenly I fell face forward, not even realizing what had happened. Diane, who was also on the platform worshiping, heard the thud and saw me on the floor. She told me later, "I asked the Lord what was happening," and the Lord said, "I am getting him out of the way!" This time I was more quietly enjoying the Father loving on me. I could hear the elders whispering to each other asking if I was okay. Another one mentioned he should go check on me to see if I had a pulse, but he quickly decided not to attempt that.

The church continued to worship, and then I heard others falling to the floor without anyone suggesting it to them. It was plain to see the Holy Spirit was in charge; there was a sovereign weightiness of the Lord in the room. Some people were hilariously laughing while others were quietly weeping. The testimonies that would follow in the weeks and months ahead were astonishing. The Holy Spirit was revealing the Father Heart of God. Many received healing deep inside their hearts.

The joy of the Lord was giving us new strength, and we were never the same. Proverbs 17:22 (NASB) says, *"A joyful heart is good medicine, but a broken spirit dries up the bones."* The yokes were being broken by virtue of the anointing of joy, which was the oil that the Lord poured on us. We witnessed firsthand the good medicine that came from the joy of the Lord. The manifestation of laughter was not the goal, but what happened during those spiritual transfusions was the glorious part that was transforming. I learned from those times of immersion of joy that joy was not only a time of refreshing, it became a weapon that I had not had before.

While in Mexico ministering, I encountered a young man who attempted to disrupt the meeting by charging toward the platform. In a demonic voice and in English, he said he was there to pluck my eyes out and kill me. My normal response would have been agitation and I would have started rebuking the demon. But this time I started to laugh as I felt the joy of the Lord rising in me from my spirit, not from my mind. My mind would have been disturbed at this young man's actions.

When he stood on the first step to the platform, through my laughter I said, "You are such a small demon, and you are through, now get out and leave him." Although no one touched him, he flew backward hitting the floor. Then some deacons dragged him to a back room.

At the end of the meeting, the young man came back in fully delivered and baptized in the Holy Spirit. That's when I found out that he didn't speak English. I saw how quickly the joy of the Lord overwhelmed the demon and it was over in maybe a minute. It was a sign and wonder to the rest of the people attending the service. Psalm 2:4 (NIV) says, *"The One enthroned in heaven laughs; the Lord scoffs at them."* The anointing breaks the yokes of bondage and the kingdom of darkness doesn't know what to do when we are not fearful or confused; when we are infused with joy of the Lord so unspeakable, the glory overwhelms the enemy.

THE CLASH OF TWO KINGDOMS

For the kingdom of God is not eating and drinking, but righteousness and peace and joy in the Holy Spirit (Romans 14:17 NKJV).

It's exciting to see that joy is part of the anointing of the Holy Spirit. The Kingdom of God is described as one of joy. The opposite of joy is fear and grief, both of which are adequate descriptions of the kingdom of darkness. When joy is present, the light of the Kingdom of God is displayed to dispel darkness that keeps people in despair and confusion. The clash of these two kingdoms become very distinct, and joy always triumphs over darkness.

Ephesians 4:30 (NKJV) says to us, *"Do not grieve the Holy Spirit of God, by whom you were sealed for the day of redemption."* To grieve is the idea of a jilted lover who was left at the altar and would not commit to marriage. If the Holy Spirt—our Advocate who has sealed us to direct us toward the day of redemption—is grieved, then the joy that comes from Him is suppressed and we quickly can feel lost and adrift. Joy is also the awareness that the Holy Spirit is always present with us.

The Kingdom of God is not about all the external things we think of kings doing, such as eating and drinking; rather, the Kingdom of God is within us. Jesus made it clear when He was facing Pilate the Roman judge. When Pilate was trying to understand who Jesus was, He answered Pilate, *"My kingdom is not of this world. If My kingdom were of this world, My servants would fight, so that I should not be delivered to the Jews; but now My kingdom is not from here"* (John 18:36 NKJV). This is a perfect picture of the clash of these two kingdoms.

The kingdom of man on earth was one of fighting for self-appointed power and influence. Jesus was referring to His Kingdom that is out of this world domain—its warfare is not flesh-and-blood fighting; its warfare is spiritual and fought in the heavenlies. Paul refers to this Kingdom as one of righteousness, peace, and joy in the Holy Spirit. This teaches us that the best warfare strategy comes from the Kingdom and operates out of joy—not fear and intimidation. Job 3:25 (NIV) says, *"What I feared has come upon me."* This is how the kingdom of darkness finds loopholes

to set up a base of operation. The devil looks for places of fear that can be exploited to send in more demons of fear to feed off the host. In contrast, the Kingdom of God builds a joyful foundation in believers that resists fear and at times attacks the strongholds of fear to bring freedom to the enslaved.

The Holy Spirit strengthens those who are filled with joy and empowers them. The very nature of God is one of joy and that's why it is a heavenly currency we need to learn how to draw upon.

> *For the weapons of our warfare are not carnal but mighty in God for pulling down strongholds, casting down arguments and every high thing that exalts itself against the knowledge of God, bringing every thought into captivity to the obedience of Christ* (2 Corinthians 10:4-5 NKJV).

Since we don't use conventional weapons of flesh and blood against an enemy of a demonic nature, our weapons must be from the Kingdom of God. Joy is not only a defensive weapon, it is also an offensive weapon.

LET NO ONE TAKE YOUR JOY

Jesus placed more emphasis on maintaining a heart of joy. Jesus uses the example of a woman giving birth. While in labor she has sorrow or pain, but as soon as she has given birth to the child, she is no longer in anguish for the joy that the child has brought into the world. John 16:22 reveals, *"Therefore you now have sorrow; but I will see you again and your heart will rejoice, and your joy no one will take from you."* Since joy is not an emotion of the soul but an empowerment in our spirit and no one can

take your joy, we are responsible to allow the joy of the Lord to rule over us.

One of the tactics of the devil is to block the joy of the Lord from ruling inside us. Since he can't take joy from our spirit, the only chance of this happening is to distract us from living from the inside out, to living from the outside in. Living for the inside means we are drawing from our spirit the eternal strength. Ecclesiastes 3:11 says He has put eternity into our hearts. Living from the inside of our spirit-led heart gives us an eternal perspective that keeps us from becoming distracted by the cares of life. The distraction happens when we are focused on everything happening to us instead of focusing on who is in us.

> *So we fix our eyes not on what is seen, but on what is unseen,*
> *since what is seen is temporary, but what is unseen is eternal* (2
> Corinthians 4:18 NIV).

The joy of the Lord is unseen and eternal, the things outside us are seen and temporary. To protect what is eternal, we must be cautious not to be distracted by the temporal issues of life. So we should be willing to test the spirits by ask a series of questions. The first being, "Where is the source of this disturbance coming from?" Second, "Is this a temporary feeling or condition that will soon pass?" And if so, "Why do I want to give it any longevity by giving it any more attention?"

THE MANDATE OF JOY

It was July 17, 1987. This date is emboldened in my mind. This was when we started Trinity Fellowship in Tyler, Texas. It was not only a starting

date, it was about the same time that I heard loudly in my heart the mandate of what my assignment would be as the founding pastor. I was asking for wisdom of how to lead the fledgling group into decades of change.

There were three things that the Holy Spirit impressed upon me that I would be responsible to carry out as a mission for the startup church. The first came to me out of Nehemiah 8:10 (NKJV), *"Then he said to them, 'Go your way, eat the fat, drink the sweet, and send portions to those for whom nothing is prepared; for this day is holy to our Lord. Do not sorrow, for the joy of the Lord is your strength.'"* This verse stood out to me as if it was written in neon lights. There are a couple of points that are important to me in response to the Lord. One for sure was to give portions to those whom nothing has been prepared. This spoke to me that we were to remember the poor and struggling families who were not a target demographic for most churches. So on day one we started handing out groceries to anyone who needed food. Today this outreach has grown into needing a warehouse and a palletized handling of products with a forklift and truck.

The second part of this verse was the importance of the joy of the Lord. What's more is that the joy of the Lord is strength. The word *strength* in Hebrew is *moed,* and intensifies the verb with much or to the maximum potential. I have found this to be so true. When joy is present while I minister, there seems to be an intensity to prophesy or the boldness to step outside of my normal. Notice that the verse does not say joy *for* the Lord, which implies a sort of zeal or passion which is fine in a soulish sort of way. The verse explicitly proclaims it is the joy *of* the Lord, meaning it belongs to and comes from the Lord. The context of this verse in Nehemiah is a prophetic word to combat the harassment of their enemy who was attempting to dissuade them from rebuilding

the walls of Jerusalem and thus interrupt the rebuilding of the temple to restore worship among the Jews.

The joy of the Lord wasn't an emotional pep talk; it was the empowering of the Lord to accomplish the mission. Over the years when I was facing a difficult time, I could go to my stronghold and spend some time meditating on the Word of the Lord to me until I could discern the joy had risen above the resistance I was facing. I would never want to go into any situation without letting the joy of the Lord bathe my spirit and ultimately flow into my soul. When Joy is present, I know the Holy Spirit will show up and show out the majesty of the presence of God.

Isaiah 12:3 (NKJV) says, *"Therefore with joy you will draw water from the wells of salvation." Salvation* is usually seen in the New Testament as *sozo,* meaning saved healed and delivered. I love the connection between the wells of salvation and joy. Joy for me is the bucket that draws up into my mind and gives me new encouragement. Learning how to dip into your spirit deep enough to draw fresh joy into your situation is a huge lesson to learn. *"I had fainted, unless I had believed to see the goodness of the Lord in the land of the living. Wait on the Lord: be of good courage, and he shall strengthen thine heart: wait, I say, on the Lord"* (Psalm 27:13 KJV). A lot of people these days struggle to see anything good in their life.

Joy is a key that gives us the ability to look beyond the chaos and see the goodness of the Lord. Joy enables us to stay focused on the vision, knowing that we will have times and issues to overcome. Joy helps us keep a constant, steady eye on the true prize. Joy is not only something we experience on earth—Heaven is filled with joy. Joy is not necessarily the absence of suffering; it the presence of God. Joy has nothing to do with our circumstances surrounding us. Joy is the deep, eternal grounding of how good God is, which invokes hope for a better tomorrow.

Since joy comes from the Lord and not from our performance, it is a constant in our lives because God never changes—He is the same historically and forever so His joy will not go away. The key is to keep joy in sight. Look for joy in everything you go through. There may not be any joy to be seen at the surface level, but ask the Holy Spirit to show you the joy in the middle of the grief. Joy is always present if we know how to look for it. We must learn to let joy take charge. One way is through praise.

THE GARMENT OF PRAISE

To console those who mourn in Zion, to give them beauty for ashes, the oil of joy for mourning, the garment of praise for the spirit of heaviness; that they may be called trees of righteousness, the planting of the Lord, that He may be glorified (Isaiah 61:3 NKJV).

Jesus read from this Scripture the precise day of the daily reading in the Temple:

So He came to Nazareth, where He had been brought up. And as His custom was, He went into the synagogue on the Sabbath day, and stood up to read. And He was handed the book of the prophet Isaiah. And when He had opened the book, He found the place where it was written: "The Spirit of the Lord is upon Me, because He has anointed Me to preach the gospel to the poor; He has sent Me to heal the brokenhearted, to proclaim

liberty to the captives and recovery of sight to the blind, to set at liberty those who are oppressed; to proclaim the acceptable year of the Lord." Then He closed the book, and gave it back to the attendant and sat down. And the eyes of all who were in the synagogue were fixed on Him. And He began to say to them, "Today this Scripture is fulfilled in your hearing" (Luke 4:16-21 NKJV).

Notice Jesus began by saying, *"The Spirit of the Lord is upon Me because He has anointed Me."* Joy is anointing that can come upon us, and one way we can yield to the anointing of joy is through praising the Lord.

Isaiah uses the picture of a garment that one would choose to put on as an act of their own will, which replaces the spirit of heaviness or the enemy of joy. Praise is recalling to your mind all the things that God has done for you beginning with salvation and all the way up to eternity. The mercy of the Lord endures forever. I have always experienced joy while I was sincerely giving thanks to the Lord with a heartfelt gratitude. Praise attracts joy, and joy puts a mantle of anointing on you. Psalm 16:11 (NKJV) says, *"You will show me the path of life; in Your presence is fullness of joy; at Your right hand are pleasures forevermore."* It's easy to know you are in the presence of the Lord because joy always accompanies His presence. Psalm 95:1 (KJV) encourages us to, *"O come, let us sing unto the Lord: let us make a joyful noise to the rock of our salvation."* The sound of praise has a joyful tone coming from those who are solid in their love for Jesus.

For me I think of Psalm 68:1 (NKJV) that says, *"Let God arise, let His enemies be scattered."* When I need to connect with the presence of the Lord, I begin to sing in the Spirit or in a heavenly tongue and allow the Holy Spirit to help me to express my love for the Lord without

asking for something or any agenda except to bathe my soul with His essence. I take strength from those times especially before I go into a meeting where I need to hear clearly the word of the Lord. Learn to linger in the presence of the Lord and let Him renew your fellowship with Him. Romans 15:13 (NIV) explains well what I am trying to convey here: *"May the God of hope fill you with all joy and peace as you trust in him, so that you may overflow with hope by the power of the Holy Spirit."*

And Galatians 5:22-25 (NKJV) tells us of the Holy Spirit's attributes:

> *But the fruit of the Spirit is love, joy, peace, longsuffering, kindness, goodness, faithfulness, gentleness, self-control. Against such there is no law. And those who are Christ's have crucified the flesh with its passions and desires. If we live in the Spirit, let us also walk in the Spirit.*

The *fruit of the Spirit* is singular, not plural—fruit not fruits. All these attributes describe what the Holy Spirit produces in a fertile heart. The first three, love, joy, and peace, are all given by the Holy Spirit to us, but the remainder of the fruit are choices. We choose to walk in longsuffering (patience), gentleness, and certainly self-control is a choice. He gives us the first three to help us with the rest of them. The word *fruit* is not something that comes from a tree necessarily; it means the result of something. For instance, the fruit of your labor is the result of you working hard. In the same way, the fruit of the Holy Spirit is the result of allowing the Holy Spirit to conform us to the blueprints that the Lord has chosen for our lives.

A Picture of Joy

I realize for most of us, trying to understand joy as a spiritual anointing as opposed to a feeling is not easy. There are two perspectives of joy: from the perspective of God and from our own perspective. Joy originates with our heavenly Father and is given to us, so in truth it is His joy that becomes our joy. For example, there are times when my wife, Diane, has asked me to do something for her. It may be that what she is asking me to do is not enjoyable, but when I see the pleasure it brings her, I feel refreshed by seeing how it brought her joy.

In the same way, we bring pleasure to the Lord when we do something in faith though at the time it is difficult and at times even stressful. In Matthew 25:23 (NKJV), Jesus assures us, *"His lord said to him, 'Well done, good and faithful servant; you have been faithful over a few things, I will make you ruler over many things. Enter into the joy of your lord.'"* In this parable of the talents, Jesus is making the point to the two faithful stewards for taking what the Lord gave them and increasing it. The servant who failed to comply with the directive to increase what was given did not receive the same blessing of entering into the joy of the Lord.

The word *joy* in Matthew 25:35 can actually be translated as *pleasure*. So here we can see the faithful stewards brought pleasure to the Lord for their obedience. They were invited to enter into the joy of the Lord. This is a very specific invitation to move from one place to another as if you invited someone to enter your home. The Hebrew language is written with not only letters but with corresponding pictographs that tell a story much like an animated film. There are three consonants that have these graphics associated with the word *joy, chet, dalet,* and *hey. Chet* is a picture of a fence or wall; *dalet* is a picture of a door; and the consonant

for *hey* is a picture of a man with his arms raised, also means to behold a great sight.

When you put these three pictures together, *joy* means in Hebrew: "Yahweh has provided a door through the wall to enter His house with open arms with delight on His face." In Hebrew culture, entering someone's house is an invitation for covenant. In this case, the joy or invitation is to pass through the wall of sin through the doorway of His Son Jesus that allows you to enter into His house and make covenant with Him. (For more on covenant see my book, *The Secret Power of Covenant*.)

"My Father's house has many rooms; if that were not so, would I have told you that I am going there to prepare a place for you?" (John 14:2 NIV). This verse from God's Word bears out with Jesus inviting us into His Father's house that is prepared for those who are in Covenant with Him. Now you can see why I see joy as a currency of Heaven. Even more, John 15:8-11 (NIV) says:

> *This is to my Father's glory, that you bear much fruit, show-ing yourselves to be my disciples. As the Father has loved me, so have I loved you. Now remain in my love. If you keep my commands, you will remain in my love, just as I have kept my Father's commands and remain in his love. I have told you this so that **my joy may be in you and that your joy may be complete**.*

It's worth noting that Jesus referred to His joy being in us, then refer-encing it being our joy. The idea is that joy will take us through difficult times since we have the same joy Jesus had on earth, and our joy is com-plete or full because His Word abides or lives inside us, which keeps joy fresh and active.

RESTORING YOUR JOY

As mentioned previously, God doesn't rescind His promise to us that we can live in His house or Covenant forever. However, there are times when drawing from the wells of salvation is difficult. In Psalm 51:10-12 (NKJV), King David is crying out to the Lord for repentance for his sin with Bathsheba: *"Create in me a clean heart, O God, and renew a steadfast spirit within me. Do not cast me away from Your presence, and do not take Your Holy Spirit from me. Restore to me the joy of Your salvation and uphold me by Your generous Spirit."* David's repentance after Nathan the prophet confronted him with the truth brought revelation to David not only of his sin, but the danger he was in of losing the presence of God and not having the Holy Spirit present with him.

Last, David prayed for restoration of the joy of his salvation. In the New Covenant, the Holy Spirit takes up a different position with us from what He did in the Old Covenant. In the Old Covenant, the Holy Spirit was more external and would come upon believers in times of need. In the New Covenant, Jesus promises us in John 14:17 that the Holy Spirit would not only be *with* us but would be *in* us. In essence the Holy Spirit moved from being around us to being in us.

Jesus also says in John 16:13 that the Holy Spirit will guide our hearts and remind us of all that Jesus has said. Jeremiah prophesied about our day, *"this is the covenant that I will make with the house of Israel after those days, says the Lord: I will put My law in their minds, and write it on their hearts; and I will be their God, and they shall be My people"* (Jeremiah 31:33 NIV). The restoration of the joy of the Lord for us today is allowing the fellowship with the Holy Spirit, which keeps joy refreshed in our hearts and minds.

Five areas to examine yourself for lost joy:

1. Has your countenance or facial expressions dropped to the point of more frowning than smiling? Read Psalm 42:11.

2. Listen to your words. Matthew 12:34 (NKJV) tells us *"out of the abundance of the heart the mouth speaks."* Has negativity taken over your language?

3. Listen to your prayers. Have they become more fear based or faith based—are they prayers of victory or of loss?

4. Check out your giving habits. Have they changed with a sense of giving out of obligation, or out of joy? Second Corinthians 9:7 (NKJV) says, *"God loves a cheerful giver."*

5. What subject do you talk about the most lately? Do you find yourself being more critical than usual or speaking more criticism than blessing?

The following is a final declaration that will help you stir up your joy, *"Oh, give thanks to the Lord, for He is good! For His mercy endures forever. Let the redeemed of the Lord say so, whom He has redeemed from the hand of the enemy"* (Psalm 107:1-2 NKJV).

The Currency
OF HIS WORD

I T'S not hard to see the reason why the Word of God is a powerful currency in Heaven. I will not attempt to place one currency above another in importance because they are all valuable to God and to you. Each currency is used in a way that will accomplish its purpose, although the blood of Jesus opens the door for all other currencies to have value and authority.

As you continue to read this book, hopefully you will learn how to deploy each one these valuable tools I call currency. Each issue or crisis you face will call for a different currency as a strategy to win the battle to take the ground you will ultimately rule from. The Holy Spirit will guide you through the arsenal that Heaven holds for you to become victorious in the Kingdom of God.

Psalm 103:20 (NASB) says, *"Bless the Lord, you His angels, mighty in strength, who perform His word, obeying the voice of His word!"* The word of God is so important that even the angels are held to His word. Understanding how angels are dispatched from Heaven to earth makes the difference between victory or defeat. Psalm 104:4 (NKJV): *"Who makes His angels spirits, His ministers a flame of fire."* Hebrews 1:14 (NKJV):

"Are they not all ministering spirits sent forth to minister for those who will inherit salvation?"

The great advantage we have over all other creation as believers in Christ is our inheritance that He purchased for us as joint heirs with Him. As heirs of His salvation, we are given angels that minister to us on His behalf. Hebrews 2:5-8 (NIV) cites:

> *It is not to angels that he has subjected the world to come, about which we are speaking. But there is a place where someone has testified: "What is mankind that you are mindful of them, a son of man that you care for him? You made them a little lower than the angels; you crowned them with glory and honor and put everything under their feet." In putting everything under them, God left nothing that is not subject to them. Yet at present we do not see everything subject to them.*

The Hebrews writer is referring to mankind as us. Jesus has placed the works of His hands on earth under us. He would never give us the huge assignment to rule here on earth without giving us the supernatural assistance of His ministers to help us. He assigns His angels to assist us in carrying out His will on earth as it is in Heaven. Jesus came to this earth as a man to overcome the enemy and place everything in the world under His feet, thereby, giving us the authority to rule by placing it under our feet.

Romans 5:17 (NKJV): *"For if by the one man's offense death reigned through the one, much more those who receive abundance of grace and of the gift of righteousness will reign in life through the One, Jesus Christ."* Angels respond to the voice of His word. It's worth noting the reference to the voice of His word; God's word has a voice and when we are praying

or declaring His word with a focused heart in faith—we are giving voice to His word. The angels are not responsive to our whims, but the voice of His word stirs the heavenly host to act inside the government and framework of the word of God.

Hebrews 4:12 (NKJV) reveals for us: *"For the word of God is living and powerful, and sharper than any two-edged sword, piercing even to the division of soul and spirit, and of joints and marrow, and is a discerner of the thoughts and intents of the heart."*

The blessings of Heaven's currency are active and alive. It's not just vocabulary or words of a language, it is as much alive as a spirit being.

AGREEMENT IN HEAVEN

For there are three that bear witness in heaven: the Father, the Word, and the Holy Spirit; and these three are one. And there are three that bear witness on earth: the Spirit, the water, and the blood; and these three agree as one (1 John 5:7-8 NKJV).

The revelation John saw concerning the agreement between Father, Son, and Holy Spirit is amazing. *Agreement* means to speak or act in the same manner or voice. The representation in Heaven is the Father, Word, and Holy Spirit. We can see that the Word represents Jesus the Son of God who is the Living Word. When we pray in the name of Jesus, we are invoking the agreement of Heaven to act on our behalf. Not only is there representation in Heaven, but there are three who agree with voice and action here on earth, which are the Spirit, the water, and the blood, which testify toward our salvation and deliverance.

When we use the Word of God (the Bible) beyond just a historical document and speak in the same Spirit in which it was written, miracles occur. It is written in 2 Peter 1:20-21 (NKJV): *"knowing this first, that no prophecy of Scripture is of any private interpretation, for prophecy never came by the will of man, but holy men of God spoke as they were moved by the Holy Spirit."* The power of the word of God is still today connected to speaking as Holy Spirit-inspired or God-breathed. There is a huge difference between a scribe who thinks it's more important to write the Scripture with every dot and stroke of the pen precisely, than to speak the Word through the inspired life of the Holy Spirit. The Word without the Spirit is just a word, but with the quickening of the Holy Spirit, the Word comes alive and is sent toward a target. It's not the repetitiveness of saying the word as a mantra, it's through the same Spirit who was there in creation to oversee its completion and accomplishment.

We cannot see the power of the Word manifest without the agreement of the Holy Spirit. Ask the Holy Spirit to reveal the depth and life of the word you are speaking, and He will add His anointing to the word, and it becomes not just a reading word but a speaking *rhema* word.

> *For as the rain comes down, and the snow from heaven, and do not return there, but water the earth, and make it bring forth and bud, that it may give seed to the sower and bread to the eater, so shall My word be that goes forth from My mouth; it shall not return to Me void, but it shall accomplish what I please, and it shall prosper in the thing for which I sent it* (Isaiah 55:10-11 NKJV).

The word is inspired and made alive by the Holy Spirit and will bring about the intended results. The disappointment for some is when they

repeat the word but do not invite the Holy Spirit into partnering with the Word.

The word without the Spirit is static and has no movement. Just as it was in creation is still true today; God the Father willed it, Jesus the Son/ Word spoke it, and the Holy Spirit moved upon it and accomplished it.

We read in Ephesians 5:26-27 (NKJV): *"Husbands, love your wives, just as Christ also loved the church and gave Himself for her, that He might sanctify and cleanse her with the washing of water by the word."* Water in Scripture has several symbolic meanings, two of which are in this verse. The context is picturing Christ and His bride, the church. Here water is seen as cleansing as expected for a bride to prepare herself for her wedding day. Also, water is used to sanctify, meaning to separate or set apart for an exclusive use. In both cases, water is used to describe the word of God that separates us from the earthly and prepares us to be sensitive to the eternal purpose. Being sanctified is being set apart or putting a boundary around the bride so nothing can pollute her from being readied for her special day. It's amazing to me how many different areas of our lives are affected by the word of God.

Living in and listening to God's word cleanses us; it is used as a weapon in our mouth, it guides us toward the will and purposes of God, and it gives us access into the throne of God. The word of God prepares us for higher levels of service. For example, Psalm 105:19 (NKJV) says, *"Until the time that his word came to pass, the word of the Lord tested him."* This verse refers to Joseph and the dream he had concerning his future. As soon as he shared his dream with his brothers, the word began to work as a catalyst toward the fulfillment. The higher the level of the word, the greater the extent and extreme working of the word to test and prepare us for its completion. Joseph was destined to go ahead of his people into Egypt.

Joseph was 17 years old when he had the dream, and for thirteen years the word tested him three different times and places. Notice it was the word doing the testing, not his brothers or Potiphar. The word is alive, always moving us toward our destiny if we don't give up and abort the mission. When Joseph was 30 years of age, he began to serve in Pharoah's court. There was another seven years of prosperity in the land before his family arrived in Egypt. The word was Joseph's foundation, and he held to his word which opened doors and shut doors all the while it was moving him toward the ultimate fulfillment of his destiny, which was to preserve his family and satisfy the covenant God had made to Abraham. God goes to great lengths to prepare us with His word, and there are no shortcuts. So, when it came time for Joseph to step into his role as the preserver of life due to the famine, he was ready and had developed compassion and sensitivity to the fear of God.

A SUMMER OF SURPRISE

I was 17 and it was the summer before I was to enter my senior in high school. I was full of excitement, looking forward to playing sports and full of wonder as to what I would do when I graduated from high school. No one in my family had attended college, so there was not much expectation except to get a job like most. I had a summer job, and I asked my boss if I could take off for a week to go to youth camp. His answer was an emphatic "No," as it was the busiest time of the year for fence building. I was disappointed because I felt a strong pull in my heart that I was to go to the camp. I thanked my boss for the job and told him that I was going to go. He said, "Don't expect the job to be here when you get back."

That youth camp became the pivotal point in my life.

It was the last night of the camp and many of my friends had received prophetic words, but nothing for me. I was sitting in the back wearing a pink shirt and set on pulling the long hair of the girl sitting in front of me. I can't say I was really engaged in the preaching. The speaker was a very austere lady name Grace Solis. She was a little scary to me. When she prophesied, she would shut one eye and point as if she had taken aim with a rifle. I can still feel that stare as I write this today.

She said, "Young man in the pink shirt in the back." I looked around to see how many other pink shirts there were in the outside pavilion. I couldn't see any others. She insisted and pointed in my direction, and said, "Stand up." With my friend pushing on me to stand up, I finally gathered the courage and stood to my feet. I felt like I was being called into the principal's office to be rebuked for pulling the girl's hair.

Then the woman turned sideways, put her one-eyed scope on me, pointed her long index finger at me, and I felt like I had a giant target on my chest. I was always taught to look someone in the eye who was talking to me. I mustered enough courage to raise my head and look, hoping she was aiming at someone else. I raised my head and caught sight of her one eye aiming right at my chest and there was no doubt she had me in her crosshairs. Her voiced boomed across the pavilion, "Young man, God's hand is upon you to preach the Gospel to the nations and your feet will stand in many places to preach without fear or favor of man. God has given you an unusual ability to make money, but the time will come when you will lay it all down and follow Him. You will become a troubleshooter in the body of Christ."

I asked my friend sitting next to me, "What is a troubleshooter?"

He replied, "I think it's someone who gets shot for causing trouble."

I though, *Oh man, I don't want that word.* I knew something had impacted me, but I just didn't know what it was. Fortunately, someone

had recorded the word and had transcribed it for me. I still have the prophecy today; the paper has yellowed but the words are etched into my memory because I read the word weekly and sometimes daily.

When I returned home, I made the decision to pursue that word. I told all my friends I was called to be a preacher and most shrugged their shoulders not really knowing what that meant. The word became the catalyst that managed my life in ways I could not even begin to imagine. Friends I had known most of my life disappeared and I found new ones who had a similar passion for the Lord. I received more clarification on the word *troubleshooter*.

Over the years I understood, like Joseph, the word I received that day led me into some strange circumstances that were tailored just for me. The chaos I had to deal with forced me to go deep into the Holy Spirit and get wisdom about what to do. The word I received that momentous evening at camp took me into times of experiencing betrayal and rejection from some I thought would be friends forever.

Today I help oversee several churches and, on many occasions, I am called upon to intervene as an arbitrator in the lives of pastors and their leadership teams. The word certainly didn't stop working until, you guessed it, I had become a "troubleshooter." It's not a job anyone really wants, but it's one that through much pain on my own and plenty of mistakes, I learned to have compassion for those going through similar difficulty, hopefully helping them avoid pitfalls along the way. The word certainly does test, but not for failure—for graduation. At each point of graduation there is a new level of authority given and a greater understanding of how to use the spiritual weapons gifted to us.

Like currency we use every day to buy food and clothing, that currency is recognized by banks and our government guarantees the value of the paper and value presented. In much the same way, the word of

God is backed up by the government in Heaven and guarantees the worth and responsiveness to His Word. Speaking the Word of God is much more than quoting Scriptures correctly, it is the spirit inside you that gives witness to the Word.

I can tell the difference when I am reading my Bible for personal edification and when the Holy Spirit highlights a particular verse, and the intensity of its worth comes out of my mouth different from when I am only reciting it.

> *And we have such trust through Christ toward God. Not that we are sufficient of ourselves to think of anything as being from ourselves, but our sufficiency is from God, who also made us sufficient as ministers of the new covenant, not of the letter but of the Spirit; for the letter kills, but the Spirit gives life* (2 Corinthians 3:4-6 NKJV).

The Old Testament was the letter of the law, and the New Testament is the Word with the Spirit. The currency I am referring to is the Word that is Spirit led and energized that causes things to be transformed. A sermon filled with Scriptures that have not been made alive by the Spirit is full of knowledge but no life. Knowledge doesn't cause Heaven to respond; it is the Word of God that speaks, and it will not return without accomplishing what it was sent to do.

THE SENT WORD OF GOD

Psalm 107:20 (NKJV) says, *"He sent His word and healed them, and delivered them from their destructions."* His Word is alive, and it can travel

distances to where and to whom it was sent, finding a landing strip to heal as in the case of the Roman soldier in Matthew 8:8 (NKJV): *"The centurion answered and said, 'Lord, I am not worthy that You should come under my roof. But only speak a word, and my servant will be healed.'"* Jesus was impressed with the Roman officer who was in command of 100 soldiers and understood authority. When Jesus offered to go to the house of his sick servant, the officer said, "Speak the word only and my servant will be healed."

Two things that stand out to me in this verse. Not only did the centurion understand the power of Jesus' authority, he also proclaimed the end result that his servant would be healed without any reservation of the outcome. The word spoken in authority must also have confidence as to the outcome. The question should be answered here as to what the sent word is. Jesus was quoting from a New Testament manuscript as a particular verse to recite in the healing of the centurion's servant. John 1:1-3 (NKJV): *"In the beginning was the Word, and the Word was with God, and the Word was God. He was in the beginning with God. All things were made through Him, and without Him nothing was made that was made."*

Pay close attention to how John proclaims Jesus the Word. In all English versions of the Bible, in John 1:1-3 the word *Word* is capitalized, referring to the Person of Jesus Christ, not vocabulary. The revelation of this is the Word-Jesus was in the beginning at creation with God, thus the verse at creation that states, *"Let Us make man in Our image"* (Genesis 1:26 NKJV). "Us" is referring to the Father, Son-Word and the Holy Spirit. Since the Living Word was present at creation, we see today that the same Word at creation is now living inside every born-again believer. First John 4:4 tells us that greater is He the Word, confirming with the Holy Spirit who is in us, than the little he, the devil, in the world.

The One present at creation spoke the Word and creation separated chaos. Just think about this for a moment, the Sent One from Heaven to earth is the Sent One in us using us to send His Word with the same faith He sent it into creation and to heal the centurion's servant. Heaven honors the Sent Word today, and that is how we learn to use the currency of Heaven of the Sent Word.

There is so much to learn from 1 John 1:3 (NKJV), *"All things were made through Him, and without Him nothing was made that was made."* Meaning, anything created was not created without Him, the Word. Everything that was created involved the Word. So if anything today needs a creative miracle, the Word must be involved. John 1:14 (NKJV) tells us, *"And the Word became flesh and dwelt among us, and we beheld His glory, the glory as of the only begotten of the Father, full of grace and truth."* Jesus the Word came in the form of a man to show we can be fully flesh and blood and live in the creative Word of God to fulfill the destiny set for our lives.

Our human nature must be retrained to act instead of react. Reaction comes from past experiences that are not always positive. We store up memories and pull from negative memory banks, causing a reaction to something someone said or something done to us. When the Word of God is dominant, we will act on the positive basis of the Sent Word, not a reaction looking in the rearview mirror. The Sent Word is creative— the reactive word is destructive. Jesus says in John 6:63 (NKJV), *"It is the Spirit who gives life; the flesh profits nothing. The words that I speak to you are spirit, and they are life."* The words are not mere language of some sort, words carry the nature of Spirit and life.

If we can adjust ourselves to distinguish between the *graphic* (written) with the *logos* of the said Word of God, we would be speaking and sending out of our spirit the *rhema*, or saying Word of God. One form is a listening level as we read the Scriptures; but when the Holy Spirit

ignites it in your spirit, it becomes a hearing Word that we speak and it becomes a saying or *rhema* word of God. We have been translated from the kingdom of darkness to the Kingdom of Jesus so we can carry the divine nature, not the fallen nature of Adam. Because we can learn to practice the divine nature and act according to His sent nature, let us not give any opportunity for the flesh to dominate our God-given heritage.

While ministering in Kentucky, I felt the prompting of the Lord to pray for anyone who had a diagnosis of cancer. Two older gentlemen came forward. I prayed over both, but one I especially felt was pulling on my faith. I noticed I had prayed over him somewhat different from the other one. I believe it was the leadership of the Holy Spirit and not my own random praying. I was not really referring to the cancer, instead I was declaring Jesus the Healer and His promise to us of healing, and of healing being the children's bread.

I flew home Monday and the pastor contacted me a few days later to let me know the man I am referring to went to his oncologist for a regular checkup. The prognosis had not been good in the previous visits. There was confusion about the scanner not working and he was told to return the next day. The doctors finally had to acknowledge they could not find any signs of the previous cancer.

I take away from this a testimony what happens when Jesus the Healer is exalted above the cancer. It's easy to lose sight of the Word being alive to heal when we instead focus on the problem and not the One whose Word is the solution. Psalm 34:1-3 (NKJV) points us to where our focus should always be:

> *I will bless the Lord at all times; His praise shall continually be in my mouth. My soul shall make its boast in the Lord; the*

humble shall hear of it and be glad. Oh, magnify the Lord with me, and let us exalt His name together.

The secret to training our brains to live in the realm of miracles is to always magnify the Lord above the circumstances we are facing. Whatever we magnify we will empower. When complaints are magnified, we will empower the enemy to take advantage of our weak position.

Let the words of my mouth and the meditation of my heart be acceptable in Your sight, O Lord, my strength and my Redeemer (Psalm 19:14 NKJV).

John 15:7-8 says, "*If you abide in Me, and My words abide in you, you will ask what you desire, and it shall be done for you. By this My Father is glorified, that you bear much fruit; so, you will be My disciples.*" The Greek word for *abide* here is *meno* and means to remain where you are; it is used to describe someone who has pitched their tent or built their house and stay on the land. The idea is to be constant, not a transitory guest. Those who are in and out, so to speak, will find it hard to live in the abiding Word because they keep moving their tent.

The circumstances you are facing do not change the effectiveness of the Word. Jesus offers a proclamation to us that if we stay and live in the dwelling of His Sent Word, we can ask what we desire, and it will be done. When we are steadfast in the realm of the Sent Word, our desires will change to fit His Word.

YOU HAVE THE BEST ATTORNEY

The divine connection between Heaven and earth is Jesus the Son of God also recognized as the Word of God. Not only the blood of Jesus bridges the gap between God and man, the Word of God also connects us to the government of God in Heaven. We have already seen how the angels are held to the Word of God and respond only to the Word, also the devil is a legalist who knows the Word as well. He will twist the word like a Leviathan, as he did in the Garden of Eden, to fit his agenda.

Remember, the first thoughts and words outside of God came from the devil, the serpent. The serpent, aka the adversary, said to Eve, "Did God really say you would die if you ate this fruit?" (see Genesis 3:1). Revelation 12:10 calls satan the accuser of the people of God. The devil knows the Word enough to deceive and trap people on legality of twisting the Word. Just as if you were in court and you had an attorney representing you and he would advise you concerning the law of that jurisdiction. The judge is bound to the law just as angels are bound to the Word of God. The Holy Spirit is our Advocate according to John 16:13, and He will guide us into all truth.

The devil tried to test Jesus with the same tactics using the Word to trap Him. In Matthew 4:3-10 the devil three times used the Word to tempt Jesus to misuse the Word of God by quoting the Word out of context and purpose. Each time Jesus answered, *"It is written."* The Word of God was used to break the misapplied purposes of the Word. John 8:32 (NKJV): *"You shall know the truth and the truth shall make you free."* There is a big difference between *knowing* the truth and just *hearing about* the truth. Knowing the truth gives you the authority to know your rights as a citizen of Heaven, carrying the currency of the heavenly realm.

Many misquote this verse by saying, *"set you free"* rather than *"make you free."* The verse is definite with the translation of *"make you free."* The difference is that *make* comes from the idea of creating freedom by knowing the truth. Truth is more than information or knowledge; Truth is the Person of the Holy Spirit. When we know the Word and its power, we are living and walking in freedom and can help others achieve freedom through being under the government of God through His Word. It's not the truth we *hear* that makes us free, only the truth we *apply*.

For example, Psalm 119:11 (NKJV) tells us, *"Your word I have hidden in my heart, that I might not sin against You."* Knowing the Word enables you to pray with targeted prayers, knowing the will of God. When the Word is obeyed, confusion disappears.

As I mentioned in the previous chapter about the Hebrew language using pictures or pictographs to translate joy, here we have a similar way to translate the word *obey*. Since obedience is the key to see the word activated, we should understand how strong it is in the Hebrew. Obey has three letters: *sheen, mem,* and *ayin. Sheen* is a picture of teeth, meaning to crush; *mem* is a picture of a turbulent sea, meaning confusion or chaos; the third letter is *ayin,* which is a picture of an eye, meaning to see or to understand. Putting these together, to obey means to crush confusion so you can understand. To obey the Word of God is to crush confusion and gain understanding.

Meditating on the Word is hugely important to renewing and cleansing the mind. To obey is the next leap in seeing the word activated because we move from a thinking word to now an application word that puts everything into motion. Hebrews 1:1-3 (NKJV):

> *God...by the prophets has in these last days spoken to us by His Son, whom He has appointed heir of all things, through whom*

also He made the worlds, who being the brightness of His glory and the express image of His person, and upholding all things by the word of His power, when He had by Himself purged our sins, sat down at the right hand of the Majesty on high.

All of creation is held together by the spoken Word of God at creation. How much more when we are obedient to His Word are we upheld in His power to succeed in what He sent us to do. Since power and life reside in the tongue, when we give voice to the Word of God, we are upholding the promises given to us individually. Marriages and families are either upheld or torn down by our adherence to giving voice to the Word of God. Psalm 119:89 (NKJV) emphatically states: *"Forever, O Lord, Your Word is settled in heaven."*

The following are four activations of the Word of God that have been settled and affirmed in Heaven and that release demonstrations on earth:

1. *Power to reveal.* Hebrews 4:12 tells us the Word is a discerner of thoughts and intents of the heart.

2. *Power to reproduce.* Matthew 13:23 (NKJV):

   But he who received seed on the good ground is he who hears the word and understands it, who indeed bears fruit and produces: some a hundredfold, some sixty, some thirty.

3. *Power to heal.* Psalm 107:20 (NKJV) says, *"He sent His Word and healed them."*

4. *Power to bind the enemy.* Matthew 16:19 (NKJV):

And I will give you the keys of the kingdom of heaven, and whatever you bind on earth will be bound in heaven, and whatever you loose on earth will be loosed in heaven.

6

The Currency
OF WORSHIP

WORSHIP is one of the most overlooked and misunderstood currencies of Heaven. When you read and study the environment surrounding the throne of God, you soon discover worship is the culture of surrounding the presence of God. For most, the term *worship* is about singing songs on a Sunday morning as a prelude before the sermon. For others, worship is about the musicality of the team leading worship and the song list they chose that day. If all we do is sing songs projected on a screen, we are only singers who are yet to experience worship. Worship existed long before the earth existed and humankind was created. Worship actually existed before we had music and knew about chord progressions to enter the sanctuary of the Most High God. Worship described through the Bible is not one of observing, but one of engagement and involvement with our entire being.

When worship moves from the pleasure of the soul to the engagement of our spirit, we cease to listen to the music and start moving into the secret place of God. In the secret place of the Most High, we are hidden and concealed by Him. Psalm 91:1-2 (NKJV): *"He who dwells in the*

secret place of the Most High shall abide under the shadow of the Almighty. I will say of the Lord, 'He is my refuge and my fortress; my God, in Him I will trust.' Notice what happens when we discover the secret place—our revelation of who the Lord is changes from believing about to speaking on His behalf. The word *shadow* here is closely translated to the word for *thoughts*. We could say that whoever has engaged in demonstrative worship will enter to a secret place with God and hears His thoughts and begins to speak as someone speaking for the Lord. Who can know the thoughts of the Lord, but those who have entered the secret place being overshadowed (thoughts of God) with His glory. In the secret place there is deposited currency that brings a wealth of revelation that opens understanding for future expenditures.

WAR OVER WORSHIP

Worship is not just activity—at its very core is the power and authority to reign. The first war before creation was set in order was over worship, and the last war to ever be fought will be over worship. This is a war that every believer needs to win inside themselves in order to enter the throne room of God.

> *And war broke out in heaven: Michael and his angels fought with the dragon; and the dragon and his angels fought, but they did not prevail, nor was a place found for them in heaven any longer. So the great dragon was cast out, that serpent of old, called the Devil and Satan, who deceives the whole world; he was cast to the earth, and his angels were cast out with him* (Revelation 12:7-9 NKJV).

This obviously wasn't a war with tanks and bullets; it was a different kind of war that did not involve flesh and blood. The word *war* in this Scripture passage is *polemos,* meaning the art of words and argument. We would say like a debate except this type of debate is not the search for the truth—rather the twisting of truth to deceive or turn someone away from the destiny and purpose of God's plan. Lucifer was convincing some of the angels to follow him by slandering God using lies to create an environment of deception.

As mentioned in Chapter 3, the same tactic was used in the Garden of Eden with Eve when the devil in the form of a serpent introduced the thought that God was not correct when He said that if Adam and Eve ate from the Tree of the Knowledge of Good and Evil they would die. The twisting of words was to create doubt concerning God's Word. The devil knew the only way he could get access to the only creation that carried the Spirit of God was to get them to disobey God, which would separate them from God's presence and glory. When the devil had succeeded in separating them from God, the glory that covered their naked bodies and the lens through which they saw each other was lifted. They now experienced *Ichabod*, meaning the "glory has departed." Immediately they ran away from the presence of God, whereas before they were drawn toward the sound of God.

Also mentioned previously but worth repeating is that God wanted Adam and Eve to confess where they were not so much by location but where they were in relationship to Him. They quickly went into blame mode for their nakedness—being out from under the covering of His glory. Adam said in essence, "That woman You gave me ate from the tree first, and she said the devil made her do it." We can see still today how people quickly blame others for their misfortune or their own disobedience to God and His Word. With the covering of the blood of Jesus and the glory of God, the devil can't do anything but try to debate with

and challenge God's word to draw us out from under His protective covering.

In 2 Corinthians 10:4-5 (NKJV) we're told:

> *For the weapons of our warfare are not carnal but mighty in God for pulling down strongholds, casting down arguments and every high thing that exalts itself against the knowledge of God, bringing every thought into captivity to the obedience of Christ.*

Some manuscripts translate the word *argument* as a stronghold. The Greek word here is *noema,* simply meaning thoughts that build a fortress in our minds. If we can control our thoughts, then every part of our life can be changed. (For more depth into this topic, read my book *The Power of Right Thinking.*) The battle or strategy of the devil is to interact with our inward dialogue. The quicker you recognize the deceptive thoughts comparing the Truth of God's Word to the twisting of the Leviathan spirit of the devil, the quicker you will be free from the intrusion of the enemy trying set up a forward base of operation in your thoughts.

We also get the word *politics* from this word translated as war. Today the world of politics is about slandering an opponent to persuade others to vote for or follow their agenda. Notice the language politicians use to encourage their constituency to follow them. They use words and phrases such as, "I'm fighting for you," which are warlike and prompt a war of words between the two candidates—followed with slander-accompanying accusations.

Worship is a calling of every believer, which also carries with it a place of authority of who will we follow. When John the Baptist was baptizing

Jesus, the voice from Heaven spoke over Jesus saying, *"This is My beloved Son, in whom I am well pleased"* (Matthew 13:17 NKJV). This was the voice of God declaring over His Son, Jesus, what is said over a son at a bar mitzvah. Let's look at the next verses as the Holy Spirit leads Jesus into the wilderness to be tested by the devil.

> *Now when the tempter came to Him* [Jesus], *he said, "If You are the Son of God, command that these stones become bread." But He answered and said, "It is written, "Man shall not live by bread alone, but by every word that proceeds from the mouth of God"* (Matthew 4:3-4 NKJV).

Take note that the last thing the Father said to Jesus His Son was, *"This is My Son,"* and the first thing the devil said in verse 3 is, *"If You are the Son of God, command that these stones become bread."* The devil using his weapons of war which are slander to question everything God says and does. The devil was trying to get Jesus to respond to his challenge to prove His identity and deity.

The last test that the devil threw at Jesus is found in Matthew 4:8-9 (NKJV) *"Again, the devil took Him up on an exceedingly high mountain and showed Him all the kingdoms of the world and their glory. And he said to Him, 'All these things I will give You if You fall down and worship me.'"* Satan's ultimate ploy all along was to get Jesus to bow and worship him. Like in the very beginning, worship depicted power and authority. To bow is to honor and submit to the one you worship. I hope you can now see that worship is about to whom we give our honor and authority. The devil knew if Jesus had bowed to him like the other angels that fell, the devil would have greater authority by dividing the Three who agree in Heaven: the Father, the Son, and the Holy Spirit. At each test

Jesus did not get into a war of words with the devil—He only quoted the Word of God.

We need to understand that the last war will be over worship. The earth will be divided in two groups before the finality of this world. The question will be who you will worship, not just sing songs about, but actively engage your whole heart, mind, and being. There will be those who will worship the beast under the influence of the dragon, and those who will worship the Lamb of God. Just as the original war over worship in Heaven brought about judgment, so also there will be judgment of those who choose to worship the beast. I think it's interesting the test is still in measuring us today over worship. My takeaway from this section, is to never take lightly worship or become solely a spectator as if you are at a concert. Ask the Holy Spirit to draw you into His presence and ultimately into the secret place.

> *You worship what you do not know; we know what we wor-ship, for salvation is of the Jews. But the hour is coming, and now is, when the true worshipers will worship the Father in spirit and truth; for the Father is seeking such to worship Him. God is Spirit, and those who worship Him must worship in spirit and truth* (John 4:22-24 NKJV).

The backstory to this Scripture passage is Jesus making contact with a woman in Samaria at a community well. Normally Jews did not venture into Samaria, but Jesus purposely went, knowing there would be a special encounter. The woman, realizing Jesus was a prophet who knew things about her that no one outside of Sychar could have known, poses a question to Jesus. Understanding He was a prophet, she could have asked Him anything. She could have asked Him, "Why haven't I been successful in marriage," or, "Why do the other women of the city

refuse to come to the well with me?" Instead, she asked Jesus, in essence, "Where are we supposed to worship?" (See John 4:19-26.)

Her question about where to worship reveals her true hunger was far greater than her social stratus in the community. She was confused that He, being Jewish, would even speak to a Samaritan much less a woman. Her tradition taught her that she had to go to Mount Gerizim, which at that time the Samaritan temple there was in ruins. She wanted to know if Mount Zion, being the place of worship for Jews, was the correct place to worship. Jesus said to her, *"The hour is coming, and now is, when the true worshipers will worship the Father in spirit and truth; for the Father is seeking such to worship Him"* (John 4:23 NKJV). This powerful statement of searching for worshipers lets me know that worship and worshipers are highly valued in Heaven.

The tradition of location was no longer a factor—only those who worship in the secret place of their heart being led by the Spirit of Truth. The word *truth* is translated as *alethia,* which means the manifest reality through the eyes of God. If we truly want to understand how God wants to be worshiped beyond our preferred style and methods, we need to ask the Holy Spirit to lead us into the truth of worship. Don't let the devil win the war over worship by distracting you with cares of life and inconvenience of time and energy. Just think, every time you turn your affections toward the Lord and worship Him, you are making a deposit into your account.

THE THRONE OF WORSHIP

Psalm 22:3 (NKJV) says, *"But You are holy, enthroned in the praises of Israel."* The Hebrew word *tahilla,* or love song of the heart, invites the

Lord to sit upon His place of justice and judge our enemies. The great benefit of being a worshiper is we can enter an intimate expression that brings us into connection with His throne. His throne represents sovereign authority and judgment. Through the *tahilla* praise He is enthroned to judge His enemies that attack us.

Hebrews 1:8-9 (NKJV) tells us, *"But to the Son He says: 'Your throne, O God, is forever and ever; a scepter of righteousness is the scepter of Your kingdom. You have loved righteousness and hated lawlessness; Therefore God, Your God, has anointed You with the oil of gladness more than Your companions.'"*

Psalm 22:22 (NIV) is a declaration: *"I will declare your name to my people; in the assembly, I will praise you."* This psalm is more descriptive of Jesus than David. It is comforting to know that Jesus is among the congregation worshiping through us to His Father. Christ is in us revealing the heart of the Father. One of His purposes for teaching His disciples was to reveal the Father to them. It helps to realize that when we are truly worshiping, we are yielded conduits through whom Jesus can worship.

Hebrews 13:15 (NKJV): *"Therefore by Him let us continually offer the sacrifice of praise to God, that is, the fruit of our lips, giving thanks to His name."* Most manuscripts translate this verse as, *"Through Jesus let us...."* A good picture of what it means to be a submitted participant of worship is to view yourself as an instrument in the hands of a skilled musician. A musician knows how to touch the strings of the instrument to bring out of the instrument the desired sound. In the same, way we can gain sensitivity to the Holy Spirit as to what the Lord wants to bring out of us as worship the throne of God.

Psalm 89:15-18 (NKJV) says, *"Blessed are the people who know the joyful sound! They walk, O Lord, in the light of Your countenance. In*

Your name they rejoice all day long, and in Your righteousness, they are exalted. For You are the glory of their strength, And in Your favor our horn is exalted. For our shield belongs to the Lord, And our king to the Holy One of Israel."

People who know or understand that the joyful sound is the sound centered on the Lord are blessed. A blessed worshiper is different from someone who only enjoys singing. True worshipers are filled with delight and joy, and their hope is anchored in eternity, not only in the life that is seen.

THOSE BORN IN ZION

Psalm 87:5-6 (NKJV) tells us, *"And of Zion it will be said, 'This one and that one were born in her; and the Most High Himself shall establish her.' The Lord will record, when He registers the peoples: 'This one was born there.'"* Zion is the mount or raised place where Solomon built the original temple and is still considered today as the sacred place of worship. Zion for us represents worship and not only a particular location of worship for the Jewish nation, but also for the heart of worship for all believers around the world. One way of interpreting these two verses is to see it in light of a birthplace. For Christians, being born in Zion is the revelation and birthing of the spirit of worship in our hearts. The writer uses the term of registering those born in Zion as if there was a birth certificate given.

Revelation 20:12 (KJV) reveals: *"And I saw the dead, small and great, stand before God; and the books were opened: and another book was opened, which is the book of life: and the dead were judged out of those things which were written in the books, according to their works."* It's important to see

that there were books, plural, that were opened whereby judgment was made. Not only the Book of Life, which would record our new birth through Jesus Christ, but other books too. There are five places in the Bible that refer to books where our actions are recorded. I am convinced that the book concerning worship will be opened about us and our obedience to worshiping the Lamb of God.

Just think for a moment about standing before the throne of God where rewards will be given out, there beside the entrance into the glory of God. There are records kept of our activity in worship or the lack thereof, based on the perspective of what the Father of Lights says is true worship, not based on location and style, but the heart of the worshiper. We normally don't take time to consider that worship will be forever and ever. Preaching and other ministries we conduct on earth will cease, but worship around the throne of God will continue without time existence.

From Revelation 13:8 (KJV): *"And all that dwell upon the earth shall worship him, whose names are not written in the book of life of the Lamb slain from the foundation of the world."* It's plain to see, worship is still the battle the antichrist is planning, to cause all whose names are not written in the Book of Life to worship the beast, and most not voluntarily. So the question some may still be asking is: Why is worship such a big deal from before the beginning of time to the end of time? The answer is simple—it is one of rulership and authority. Who we worship voluntarily from a sincere heart is granted submission over our life. That is why the devil was insistent upon Jesus bowing down to him. When we worship, we are relinquishing our rights to another. There are many who would never consider they are worshiping anything related to the devil. The devil will take anything that leans his direction, including being mediocre about worshiping Jesus alone. The power of the currency of worship is backed up by the value that Heaven gives to it, which is

eternal without end. So, you can see when you are worshiping the Lord Jesus Christ you are submitting your life and all you represent to Him, and rejecting at the same time the kingdom of darkness rule. There is no middle ground of indifference here. Whether you can sing a note or even if you are tone deaf, you can be a worshiper in spirit and truth.

Anytime in Scripture when something is measured, it's because there are rewards that will either be added to you or taken from you. Matthew 25 records Jesus giving the parable of the talents. A talent was a measure or weight of money. In the parable there was an accounting of what was given to three different servants. Each one was given an amount based on their ability, and I assume from their past performance of handling things of value. Two of the servants invested for the purpose of increase; the third one was somewhat ambivalent about his responsibility and buried what he had been given.

When the owner returned the two who invested their talents were rewarded with increase. The one who did nothing was rewarded with losing the potential he could have had. Not all rewards are for increase; how we live our lives now determines whether we will be rewarded with increase or be rewarded with loss.

Worship will be measured when we come before the judgment seat of Christ, the *bema* seat.

> *Then I was given a reed like a measuring rod. And the angel stood, saying, "Rise and measure the temple of God, the altar, and those who worship there. But leave out the court, which is outside the temple, and do not measure it, for it has been given to the Gentiles. And they will tread the holy city underfoot for forty-two months"* (Revelation 11:1-2 NKJV).

The message is clear, the angel was instructed to measure the temple of God and the worshipers within, but those outside were not to be measured for they will not inherit the Kingdom of God.

This understanding causes me to be much more conscious concerning worshiping the Lord and much more intentional and not so casual in giving attention to my birthright as a worshiper. You are depositing in Heaven something that the Lord thinks should be measured and rewarded, and it will not be stolen from you. The lack of attentiveness to our time on earth as a worshiper will also be measured. The temporary is easily used to distract or steal our energy and time so there is nothing left over for things that are eternal.

> *If then you were raised with Christ, seek those things which are above, where Christ is, sitting at the right hand of God. Set your mind on things above, not on things on the earth. For you died, and your life is hidden with Christ in God* (Colossians 3:1-3 NKJV).

Eternity was been built into our being at creation, but the immediacy of the moment can cause us to put off what has been rewarded for time without end. Any reward we receive here on earth is at best temporary, for a couple of decades at best—but eternity has no expiration stamp. As you can see, I am passionate about helping people invest into eternity, which is beyond anything we could imagine or even hope for. Hebrews 11:6 describes God as One who rewards or gives remuneration to those who pursue Him—and being a worshiper is certainly being in pursuit of Him.

Matthew 6:20-21 (NKJV) tells us to: *"lay up for yourselves treasures in heaven, where neither moth nor rust destroys and where thieves do not*

break in and steal. For where your treasure is, there your heart will be also." Since the heart sets a standard for what we consider our treasure, it takes the Holy Spirit to retrain the heart to see more from an eternal perspective. Likewise, we are to: *"Keep your heart with all diligence, for out of it spring the issues of life"* (Proverbs 4:23 NKJV). *Issues* is translated as the pathway or conduit of our destiny. We must always question our own heart, our inner spirit, to make sure we are setting a good path for ourselves eternally.

SING TO THE LORD A NEW SONG

Six times in the Old Testament and New Testament we are encouraged to "Sing unto the Lord a new song." The meaning of *new* in these verses means either fresh or original. I have witnessed this many times when singing unto the Lord spontaneously without a premeditated thought as to the words I sing. I would hear them at the same time everybody listening to me were hearing them. It was a new or original song that always released something fresh into the atmosphere.

On one such occasion, I was invited to speak on my book, *The Power of Blessing.* When I entered the sanctuary of the church, I could easily see that worship was only a prelude to the sermon, even though it was a good-sized church. The service opened without any prayer and one person playing keys led two songs rather quickly, and then I was introduced. It was my first time being there, so I took a minute to share a bit of what I was believing for in the series of meetings I was invited to present there.

I felt like I was on stage to do a magic act, to pull a rabbit out of a hat, while everyone looked on in unbelief. I did the best I could to share the Scriptures, to no avail. It was as if there was a deaf and dumb spirit that

captured the people. I even tried some funny anecdotal stories to break the iceberg that was between us, but all I received back were blank stares as if to say, "When is the real entertainment coming to the stage?" I had never been in a place that was so dead, inexpressive. I was exhausted after the first ten minutes, which seemed like an hour. Under my breath I whispered to the Holy Spirit, "What do You want me to do?" I heard clearly the Lord say, "Sing to Me a new song."

I thought, *Wow, I've given them my best stuff and they weren't impressed, so why would they would be touched with me singing?* I knew I had tried everything without any signs of movement. I knew I couldn't do any worse than the first ten minutes. So, I shut my eyes and set my heart on the Lord and started singing a love song to Jesus as if He and I were the only ones in the room. The song was filled with spontaneous words I had not sung before much less a melody I had heard previously. I continued to sing of His majesty and His greatness and mercy. It probably was two minutes at the most, but I was fully lost in the moment; caught up with my Lord, and what was happening or not happening to those listening was less important to me.

When I opened my eyes, I saw a few people kneeling at their chairs while others were standing with hands lifted. I could sense there was movement in the air as if someone had finally turned on a fan and the air was being stirred and refreshed. I just kept singing as the Holy Spirit did the rest. There was an amazing freedom for the remainder of the week.

There is something about singing a spontaneous song to the Lord that breaks through even a religious wall. The Holy Spirit is released in a more powerful way when we magnify Jesus, the One who opened the door into the heavenlies. I was reminded of the verse in Philippians 3:3 (NKJV), *"For we are the circumcision, who worship God in the Spirit, rejoice in Christ Jesus, and have no confidence in the flesh."* I could see the

change in the room; tangibly God was being worshiped in the Spirit instead of just being sung about in the third person. Worship was targeted when I sang to the Lord as opposed to singing for the purpose of the audience of the room.

Psalm 48:10 (NKJV): *"According to Your name, O God, so is Your praise to the ends of the earth...."* Simply put, this means that God manifests Himself in the same way His name is praised. The ancient rabbis believed God would reveal Himself through His name. For instance, if they praised His name as Jehovah Rapha, the God who healed them, they would see His glory manifested through the name they declared Him to be. In the same way as I sang the song that revealed the majesty and mercy of God, the amazing transformation of the atmosphere was evidenced, and the deaf and dumb spirit that captured the people began to leave so that the message that evening could be heard in their spirits. It was useless to try and speak to a crowd who were in a spiritual stupor. The Holy Spirit came and manifested the majesty of the King and broke off the people's religious chains. I enjoyed years of fellowship in returning to this sweet church.

THE SOURCE OF WORSHIP

Ezekiel 47:1 (NKJV) tells us:

> *Then he brought me back to the door of the temple; and there was water, flowing from under the threshold of the temple toward the east, for the front of the temple faced east; the water was flowing from under the right side of the temple, south of the altar.*

Ezekiel receives this vision of flowing water in a critical time for the Jewish people. Ezekiel had been in Babylon exile for twenty-five years when he wrote this powerful vision of hope. The temple in Jerusalem was in ruins, and most of the people were taken into captivity due to their idolatry and lack of obedience to God's commands. Ezekiel sees a river coming from the threshold or doorway of the temple. This vision was not a vision of rebuilding the Jerusalem temple, it was a heavenly vision.

Besides hope for restoration, the river was a message of restoring worship to the people of God. The temple was a symbol of people gathering around the presence of God. The *"flowing"* represents the flow of worship and the life that comes when water is flowing. Cities are built around rivers. The water from rivers are life-sustaining. Rivers represent flowing water, which is always fresher than water that is not moving and becomes stagnant. It is important to take notice of the source or the beginning of the river. This river began from inside the temple of God. True worship begins from the throne of God and flows down to us, and we get to give it back to Him.

It takes the love of God for us to be able to love God, otherwise we could only love Him with friendship or *phileo* love. Romans 5:5 (NKJV) says, *"Now hope does not disappoint, because the love of God has been poured out in our hearts by the Holy Spirit who was given to us."* It takes the Holy Spirit to show us how to love God. In the same way, it takes the Holy Spirit for us to worship God in the way He wants us to worship.

In the Ezekiel vision, notice the farther the river is from the temple the deeper the water becomes. In most natural rivers the farther the river is from its source, the shallower it becomes and less forceful—but with the river of God, it becomes deeper until it is waters to swim in. Wherever the river goes, life springs up. The description of this river brings fishermen from various parts to the river to fish. Fishing is a symbol of

evangelism and revival. So where worship is allowed the free course of the Holy Spirit, there is movement of revival taking place. The places that hinder the river flow, swamps are created and nothing can live in stagnant water.

True worship doesn't originate from a platform of musicians as they pour it out to the congregation. True worship originates from the throne of His sanctuary in Heaven down to us upon the people who will allow the free expression of the Holy Spirit to flow through them. I am thankful when musicians flow with the river of God.

The following Scriptures depict this flow beautifully:

Revelation 22:2 (NKJV): *"In the middle of its street, and on either side of the river, was the tree of life, which bore twelve fruits, each tree yielding its fruit every month. The leaves of the tree were for the healing of the nations."*

Ezekiel 47:12 (NKJV) gives a similar description of fruitful trees along the river and the healing properties as the flows from the sanctuary of God: *"Along the bank of the river, on this side and that, will grow all kinds of trees used for food; their leaves will not wither, and their fruit will not fail. They will bear fruit every month, because their water flows from the sanctuary. Their fruit will be for food, and their leaves for medicine."*

John 7:37-38 (NKJV): *"On the last day, that great day of the feast, Jesus stood and cried out, saying, 'If anyone thirsts, let him come to Me and drink. He who believes in Me, as the Scripture has said, out of his heart will flow rivers of living water.'"*

This type of worship is the currency Heaven will back up.

The Currency
OF BLESSING

IT may seem unusual to some readers for me to include blessing as a currency that Heaven would recognize or give authority to. The reason why it sounds somewhat different is because for most of us the definition of blessing includes the idea of material accumulation. We use the term to explain that we are doing well because we are blessed, and in some contexts that could be true.

In the context of what Heaven considers blessed has nothing to do with financial security or how many cars you might own. The biblical definition for blessing has more to do with speaking or declaring something the way God sees a matter and how we speak about it. Blessing in the Greek New Testament is *eulogia* where we get our English word *eulogy*, which means to praise or speak well of someone. 1 Peter 3:8-9 (NIV) says:

> *Finally, all of you, be like-minded, be sympathetic, love one another, be compassionate and humble. Do not repay evil with evil or insult with insult. On the contrary, repay evil with blessing, because to this you were called so that you may inherit a blessing.*

Blessing is understood by declaring the way God intends something to be—instead of saying what it appears to be at the moment. In Luke 6:28 (NKJV) Jesus says, *"Bless those who curse you, and pray for those who spitefully use you."* There is a difference between truth and facts. Facts are what things appear to be, but truth triumphs over facts. You can choose to live by the facts or live by the truth. For instance, a doctor may say you have six months to live, which may be a scientific fact, but the truth is what the Word of God says. Truth is the Person named the Holy Spirit. The truth is, *by the stripes of Jesus you are healed* (see Isaiah 53:5; 1 Peter 2:24). We are not to live by bread alone but by every word the proceeds from the mouth of God (see Deuteronomy 8:3; Matthew 4:4). Truth comes from the mouth of God; facts can be temporary when we start declaring the way God intends the situation to turn out.

Most people spend their time repeating the facts instead of blessing their body to be what God intends their body to be, which is *not* a sickly fact of science. You have a body you can either bless or curse. First Corinthians 6:19 (NKJV) says, *"Or do you not know that your body is the temple of the Holy Spirit who is in you, whom you have from God, and you are not your own?"* If you bless your body as a temple of the Lord, then you are in agreement with God's intentions for your body. Psalm 139:14 tells us that we are fearfully and wonderfully made and marvelous are God's works. Blessing your own body means calling your body back into alignment to God's original intentions of His creation for you.

The reason Heaven sees blessing as a currency is because it releases the "Word of the Lord." Notice 1 Peter 3:8-9 is very specific in not returning evil for evil; we are to instead give blessing to replace the evil or reviling words that come out of a mouth that is agreeing with the devil. The devil is the accuser, the curser of people. Blessing cuts off the intentions of the devil—blessing is our weapon that resists his plans. This Scripture passage also tells us that we are called to bless in the same way we

are called into a gifting; and by practicing the gift of blessing, we then inherit blessing. Inherited blessing is living under the word of the Lord that God declares over your life and family.

There are those who seem to live under a curse and never seem to prosper or experience any good fortune. It could be that they have not discovered the inheritance of blessing. If you have read my book *The Power of Blessing*, you will remember my account of how my life was changed forever when I discovered the revelation of blessing.

My wife, Diane, and I were driving on Interstate 30 in Dallas, Texas, headed to a meeting. Traffic was typical for the Metroplex, and if that wasn't enough, it was during 5 o'clock rush hour traffic. Suddenly, a young man in a small truck decided to cut in front of me and almost hit my right front fender. I slammed on my brakes and what came out of my mouth was something I wasn't proud of—in fact, my mother would have washed my mouth out with soap. I blurted out, "Idiot!" Diane, who sounds very much like the Holy Spirit, said to me, "Pardon me, what did you say?" I sheepishly said, "Well, he is."

To my surprise I realized I was having an inner dialogue with the Holy Spirit. I heard the Lord say, "Why did you just call Me an idiot?" Strange as it sounds, this internal conversation was straightforward, and I knew I had been busted. I replied to Him in my mind's thoughts, *I didn't call You an idiot.* And before I could finish my defense, He quoted James 3:9 (NKJV), *"With it we bless our God and Father, and with it we curse men, who have been made in the similitude of God."* I knew I had no leg to stand on when He was quoting Scripture to me. The final blow was when He said Matthew 25:40, *"As you have done it to the least of these you have done the same to Me."*

The message sunk deep into my spirit. What started out as a moment of a poor choice of words in the middle of rush hour, became a personal

life-changing message from God to me. I quickly repented all the while this was going on inside my heart, and then I heard the Lord say, "Now, bless him." I flippantly said, "Bless ya." That would not be sufficient. Then God said, "No. Bless him the way you want to be blessed." I thought to myself, *Well now, that's a completely different issue.* So I thought for a moment and the words began to flow. I started by declaring, "You are a son of promise, and you will experience the fullness of the presence of God. I bless you with long life and safety for you and your family." The only way I can explain to you what happened next is simply to say, I felt the pleasure of the Lord flowing through my physical body. It was as if all the chemistry of my brain, including endorphins, were flooding my entire being. I felt euphoric. I realized how much joy the Lord received when I was blessing instead of stating my negative opinion about someone I didn't even know.

From that moment on I wanted more of that joy, so I started blessing every situation that I encountered, even the ones that seemed there was no way for it to be turned around—and then I would see the miracle happen. Blessing really does work, and Heaven responds to invoking the very nature of the Lord into every circumstance. The way I bless others is the same way I am blessing Jesus. Because blessing is declaring the way God sees things, then cursing is the opposite of blessing. I'm not talking about cussing, which is bad too, I am speaking of cursing people or things that God has blessed. Cursing is saying or declaring something to be in a lower place than what God intends for them to be. In His prayer recorded in Matthew 6:10, Jesus asks that the Lord's will be done on earth as it is Heaven.

We know that the accuser was cast out of Heaven and was cast down to earth. We are living in the place where the god of this world blinds people through cursing and planting in their minds the words to curse one another (2 Corinthians 4:4). Cursing is the nature of our adversary.

Our warfare is against the spirit of cursing, and blessing is the weapon that cursing cannot overcome. Blessing is more than flattering statements, it is sharing the heart of God through His lens, not through the evil eyes of the devil. Evil is bound up in the heart of fallen humans, blessing comes in the opposite spirit to destroy the work of the devil. James 4:7 (NKJV) says for us to *"submit to God. Resist the devil and he will flee from you."* The word *resist* here means to replace with the opposite word. The way we can resist the devil after submitting to God is to replace cursing with blessing.

I was teaching in a Bible school about blessing, and the office manager of a company said she wasn't too sure what I was saying would work, in her case. She and the owner had been at odds for a good while, and she was sure she was going to be fired. She described the environment of the office and admitted she had done her share of cursing the boss in front of the other staff. I told her that cursing had set an atmosphere that was resistant to any favor she would receive. I challenged her to try something for at least a week, using blessing as a replacement for the cursing environment she had created with the other employees.

The next day was Monday, and she began by repenting to God for all the cursing and accusations she had gossiped to other workers. Before any of the staff or bosses had arrived that day, she went through the building blessing the boss and thanking the Lord for the source from which she derived her income. She continued blessing the other workers when the opportunity would arise. Not even a week passed before she saw a positive change in the office. She first noticed her attitude toward her boss began to soften and others saw the change in her as well.

On Friday her boss called her into his office and asked her to shut the door. She just knew the ax was coming and she was going to be fired. His first words to her were acknowledging that neither of them cared much

for each other, but he told her something had changed recently and he wanted her to stay on as office manager. He also said that he had been withholding a raise from her that she had coming two months ago, so he was going to give her the raise retroactive from two months previous. She was so excited to let me know how dramatic her work environment had changed by doing only one thing differently—changing from a mouth full of cursing to one full of blessing.

SET BEFORE YOU—LIFE AND DEATH

Deuteronomy 30:19 (NKJV) is a verse worth serious contemplation: *"I call heaven and earth as witnesses today against you, that I have set before you life and death, blessing and cursing; therefore, choose life that both you and your descendants may live."* This promise is given to us and affects generations—our choices are clear. Moses connects blessing with life and cursing with death. It boggles the imagination when we consider how much we may have destroyed using the vocabulary of darkness—when we have the choice to speak words of life. We have the choice to bless our marriage or we can curse it. We are responsible for the environment we create. Our families depend on us getting this right. God says we are to choose life, which brings blessing to us and our descendants.

Proverbs 18:21 (NKJV) *"Death and life are in the power of the tongue, and those who love it will eat its fruit."* When you consider the strong language the Word of God uses to describe the power we hold in our mouth, it is sobering. We have choices to make every day and many times a day. If you picture the devil laughing at you when you have chosen to put someone down in a lower place than what God intends, that may make you think twice the next time your are tempted to be rude or

antagonistic. Many times instead of resisting the devil, we allow evil to use us as pawns to curse, to be courier pigeons for his loathsome ways. None of us are perfect all the time to remember to bless. Human nature is to return evil for evil and insult for insult. The fleshly strategy is to fight fire with fire or in this case flesh with flesh. But we can make every effort to speak life, not death.

I grew up in a family that made an art form out of cutting sarcastic remarks. Especially the males of the family found sport in finding ways to make my sisters or mother look foolish. It all seems so strange to me now, but we insulted each other until someone became wounded enough to back down, and the one still standing felt proud of their wit and arsenal of insults. If someone's feelings were hurt, we would naively say, "I was only kidding," as if to make the other person look weak for feeling the pain.

When it came time for Diane to meet the family, I was a little concerned how they would act toward her and might see her as a fresh target. I was hoping everyone would put away their hillbilly charm while she was visiting. Diane didn't grow up with brothers and sisters, she was very refined and polite and kind.

When I came through the door with Diane for that special moment, the first greeting to me was, "Hello, ugly, how're you doing?" Though I had not been living near my family for a long time, my default reply kicked in rather quickly and I said, "Hello, uglier than I!" Diane's face said volumes. I had forgotten she was not accustomed to our barnyard decorum. She said, "What are you all doing to each other?" It was the shock on her face that caused my family to reevaluate our tradition in light of the Word of God. There was no doubt we loved each other and were always supportive of one another, but we had a blind spot that needed to be removed so we could break some generational curses.

Since we were wanted to please the Lord, it was not a hard sale—retraining our brains to react differently toward one another was the more difficult part. We all agreed that coarse and harsh jesting was not an excuse to be disobedient to the Word of God. After some time of transitioning from bad humor to one of blessing, some of my siblings shared how they had been hurt by the cutting remarks, even though said in jest. Nevertheless, it stung and remained in their memory banks, questioning if they were really loved.

The good report—we now have more of a testimony of God's transformation than anyone still carrying the pain and rejection from the family tradition. And we have come to realize that sometimes when we curse someone, it may have a boomerang affect—both people are hurt by negative speech. We really are our "brother's keeper," and can't just brush off a hurtful comment by saying the person shouldn't have taken what was said so personally. Our words have a landing strip in another's heart that we should take seriously.

Proverbs 26:2 (NKJV) says, *"Like a flitting sparrow, like a flying swallow, so a curse without cause shall not alight."* The point of this proverb is that just like when a bird leaves a nest, it looks for another place or nest to land. A curse must find another place of cursing before it can land. For instance, someone who is a curser becomes a landing strip for other cursings. We tend to attract spirits similar to the ones we are carrying. In many cases, spirits familiar to a family are based upon their actions of agreement.

We see this clearly with Jesus in John 14:30 (NKJV) when He says: *"I will no longer talk much with you, for the ruler of this world is coming, and he has nothing in Me."* Jesus was telling His followers what was going to happen to Him, and up front Jesus said, "The demonic forces of the world will try to take Me, but because there is nothing in Me that agrees or resonates with them, they are powerless." This truth played out in

John 18:4-8, in the Garden of Gethsemane, as the Roman soldiers came to take Jesus. Three times Jesus asked them, *"Whom are you seeking,"* and they responded, *"Jesus of Nazareth."* When Jesus answered saying, *"I am He,"* the soldiers fell down all three times. The reason they had no power over Jesus was because the spirit in them did not resonate with the Spirt of God in Jesus.

A curse cannot have power over you if you are not practicing cursing, which gives them access to you. Galatians 6:7-8 (NKJV) says: *"Do not be deceived, God is not mocked; for whatever a man sows, that he will also reap. For he who sows to his flesh will of the flesh reap corruption, but he who sows to the Spirit will of the Spirit reap everlasting life."* This is the law of reciprocity or the principle of return. One who is sowing cursing will see the fruit of cursing. Either the spirit of darkness is sowing seeds toward your future return on what you invested, or the Kingdom of God is returning blessing from your seed of blessing.

If you don't like the fruit you have been reaping, you must change the seed you are sowing—that is a biblical law as sure as the law of gravity. Hoping it will change doesn't cause change to your circumstances, only by changing the seed of cursing to the seed of blessing will you see change.

> *Let no corrupt word proceed out of your mouth, but what is good for necessary edification, that it may impart grace to the hearers. And do not grieve the Holy Spirit of God, by whom you were sealed for the day of redemption* (Ephesians 4:29-30 NKJV).

The apostle Paul uses strong language to explain cursing. The *corrupt* is from the Greek word *sapros,* which means putrid, decaying,

or even a foul odor. In essence he is saying, when we use foul, putrid words to express our views of someone, we are sowing what would make someone sick. If that is not enough, Paul finishes the thought with, *"Do not grieve the Holy Spirit of God, by whom you were sealed for the day of redemption."* Not only is cursing sickening to others, but cursing grieves the Holy Spirit. Grieving the Holy Spirit is used here to describe someone who is engaged to be married and then jilted at the altar. Another way to say grieving the Holy Spirit, is to liken it to a broken engagement.

The apostle Paul writes in Romans 12:14 (NKJV): *"Bless those who persecute you; bless and do not curse."* Paul bluntly says don't curse; and even when people persecute you and seemingly don't deserve blessing, we are told to bless. By doing so we are coming in the opposite spirit, thus disarming the intent of the curser.

James 3:4-5 (NKJV) tells us, *"Look also at ships: although they are so large and are driven by fierce winds, they are turned by a very small rudder wherever the pilot desires. Even so the tongue is a little member and boasts great things. See how great a forest a little fire kindles!"* The Bible describes the tongue as a small member of the body, yet it sets the direction for our lives. This is obviously a symbolic way of choosing the direction of life by what comes out of our mouth.

And Luke 6:45 (NKJV) says, *"A good man out of the good treasure of his heart brings forth good; and an evil man out of the evil treasure of his heart brings forth evil. For out of the abundance of the heart his mouth speaks."* The real culprit is not the tongue but the heart.

The heart is our mind and intellect, which we normally call our soul. From the soul we decide if we are going to be offended and retaliate in like kind, or if we will choose to extinguish the fiery darts of cursing through blessing. The soul stores up memories and thoughts from past

periences, whether helpful or harmful, and they make up the abundance of the heart.

The key is to be filled with the Spirit, speaking under the influence of the Holy Spirit and letting the abundance of the heart be filled with blessing, which is seeing through the eyes of the Lord. Whatever we feed the soul, the soul will give back in like kind. The old saying is true, "Garbage in, garbage out." This adage became popular when computers became common in the average home. People were sometimes surprised at what came out of their computer files. They had to be reminded that what went into the computer is what came out. If you have ever been surprised at what "garbage" came out of your mouth, now you know that the same had been input into your soul at some point. Thankfully, the Holy Spirt helps us clean up the clutter of the soul so we won't be caught off guard at what erupts from some old cursings.

THE HEALING THROUGH BLESSING

I still am thrilled to see the changes that come when people catch revelation of the power of blessing. I was just finishing up a conference near Houston, Texas, when a pastor friend of mine asked if I would counsel with a man before I left. I explained that I had to be in another town in just a few hours and not much time to drive. He pleaded with me, and being a friend, I acquiesced. I asked if he knew the man and he shook his head no. Well, since I said yes, I proceeded to talk with the man. The man explained that he had been overseas working as a contractor most of the year and had not spent much time at home. His question for me, "How can I stop my wife from divorcing me?" Apparently she was at the lawyer's office as we were speaking.

Before I could get a sentence out, he started describing their relationship, saying that he really didn't love her and that she wasn't much help with anything, she was very needy, and, "Oh yeah, she's just like her mother." He took a breath, so I jumped in by saying, "Well, it sounds like your problem is solved since you don't want to be married anyway." He quickly got heated with me and said, "No one is going to divorce me." While looking him straight in the eye I said, "Sir, you have the wife you bless and you have the wife you curse—and it sounds to me like you have created the wife you have been cursing."

I could tell the truth angered him and he leaned in toward me and said, "I have studied martial arts with mind control, and I can pick you up and throw you against that wall." I replied, "I have studied the Bible and I can cast that out of you."

We stared at each other for a bit, and I finally said, "I have to hit the road." I did however as a parting gift, give him some CDs I had taught on the "Power of Blessing." A few months later I was back in the Houston area ministering, and the same man walked up to me with a different countenance and asked, "Do you remember me?" I thought to myself, *Yes, I remember you, you're that Judo mind-meld guy.* I said, "Yes, I remember you."

With a smile on his face, which puzzled me, he said, "I want you to meet someone." He motioned for a woman to come near us. I thought to myself, *He worked fast and already has a new wife.* He said, "This is my wife of thirty years and I wanted her to meet you." I'm not often struggling for words, but I was speechless.

Then he said, "After you left that day, I started listening to the CDs you gave me while she was at the lawyer's office. I started to realize that my cursing her was the reason she was reacting the way she did toward me, so when she came home and stepped inside the door, I said to her,

'I'm sorry for the way I've treated you.' Then I started to bless her in the way I learned from the CDs. I told her, 'You are my help meet God gave to me as a covenant partner, and you are the joy of my heart, and I will love you the rest of your days in the way the Lord would have me love you.'"

I was watching her face as he was telling me his story to see if she was agreeing with what he had just told me. Her face was lit up like a streetlamp. She smiled and said, "I can't really say that I have ever truly loved him, but when he said those things to me, it was if the words were tangible and they hit me right in my heart. It felt as if liquid love was flowing through my body, and it feels like we have been on a honeymoon for months."

I was blown away at the change I witnessed. I realized that blessing not only changes the one he was blessing, but the change started with him first. Many times, even if you don't see the change in the one you have targeted to bless, you will notice the change in your own heart as the abundance overflows into every area of your life.

BLESSING BRINGS A NAME CHANGE

In Genesis 32 we read the interesting story of Jacob, who had been alienated from his brother Esau. Esau was the elder brother who sold his birthright for a bowl of soup at a moment of weakness. Jacob and Esau had been separated for over twenty years when God put it into Jacob's heart to return to the country and the family he had left. Word had it that Esau was coming fast and furious to meet Jacob. Due to Esau's previous deception, Jacob's first thoughts were that Esau was coming to seek revenge. Jacob, out of fear, divided his wealth and family into

two different groups so at least some of them would survive. Jacob called upon the name of the Lord, reminding God it was His idea for Jacob to return to his homeland. Jacob decided to appease him by sending on ahead of them to detect Esau's intentions.

Genesis 32:24-28 (NKJV) describes the events leading up to an unusual encounter with the Lord:

> *Then Jacob was left alone; and a Man wrestled with him until the breaking of day. Now when He saw that He did not prevail against him, He touched the socket of his hip; and the socket of Jacob's hip was out of joint as He wrestled with him. And He said, "Let Me go, for the day breaks." But he said, "I will not let You go unless You bless me!" So He said to him, "What is your name?" He said, "Jacob." And He said, "Your name shall no longer be called Jacob, but Israel; for you have struggled with God and with men, and have prevailed."*

Jacob was alone and he wrestled with a Man. The word *wrestle* is a Hebrew word meaning *torch*. At first, it's difficult to make a connection with *torch* and *wrestling*. To wrestle one must come in close. The battle is to shine the light or torch and to pull the other into the light or, we could say, the light of the truth. Some rabbinical sages say the wrestling was the pull between the body or material things of life and the heart representing the spiritual side of life. The torch or wrestling was to show the greater good.

For Jacob to be blessed, he had to confess his name, which meant trickster and deceiver. He could not be blessed until his name was changed to Israel, which represents a character change; one who has prevailed with God. Notice blessing had to show how God was viewing Jacob, not

based on the facts of his past, but was now prophetic, declaring who God intended him to be. God chose to birth a nation out of a blessing named Israel, one who prevailed with God. The end of the story is wonderful with the restoration of his relationship with his brother. The currency of blessing has the ministry of reconciliation as part of God's intentions on earth as it is in Heaven.

THE CURSE OF UNCOVERING

And Noah began to be a farmer, and he planted a vineyard. Then he drank of the wine and was drunk and became uncovered in his tent. And Ham, the father of Canaan, saw the nakedness of his father, and told his two brothers outside. But Shem and Japheth took a garment, laid it on both their shoulders, and went backward and covered the nakedness of their father. Their faces were turned away, and they did not see their father's nakedness (Genesis 9:20-23 NKJV).

When Noah awoke and knew what his younger son had done to him, he pronounced a curse upon Ham and his family. He cursed Canaan (Ham's son) and blessed Shem and Japheth (Noah's sons who covered his nakedness), asking that God enlarge their tents, meaning their families and possessions (see Genesis 9:24-27).

The important point of this story is that when we are quick to uncover people for the purpose of making them appear vulnerable or shameful, it brings about a penalty or a curse. The two sons who covered their father's nakedness was given blessings. It is the job of the Holy Spirit to uncover

what needs to be uncovered. I'm not talking about public corruption and fraud, which should be uncovered. I'm referring to uncovering someone to make them look compromised for the sake of defaming the person. If this is the intent, then there is a recourse of return cursing.

Notice Noah was in his tent, some studies even indicate he was with his wife at the time. Noah was not out in public exposing himself, but Ham's motive was to expose him to his two brothers. First John 5:16 (NIV) says, *"If you see any brother or sister commit a sin that does not lead to death, you should pray and God will give them life. I refer to those whose sin does not lead to death. There is a sin that leads to death. I am not saying that you should pray about that."*

We are encouraged to ask for life or the help of the Holy Spirit to convict them of their sin so they might turn away from sin. We are *not* encouraged to shout someone's sin from the rooftop to point out their sin from the motive of exposing their weakness and showing our self-righteousness. The sin unto death could be a hardened unrepentant person who consistently continues in sin or one who has blasphemed the Holy Spirit and whose heart is unfeeling toward God.

I believe there are three levels that the Holy Spirit works on us to repent so we are spared shame and ridicule. The first level of repentance is when the Holy Spirt comes to the secret place of our heart. There we feel conviction and remorse that leads us to privately repent and turn from the sin.

The second level is when the first level doesn't get results and the individual continues without responding to the private prompting. In the second level the Lord may send someone to us as in the case when Nathan the prophet approached David over his adulterous affair with Bathsheba. Nathan shares a parable with David, and David responded

that he would kill (2 Samuel 12:1-5) such a man who would steal another man's sheep. David repented, as we read in Psalm 51.

The third level is much more revealing of the sin. This is when it is uncovered publicly and there is no way to hide from it. Over the years we have seen leaders who I believe were confronted by the Holy Spirit and after each barrier they refused to heed—then out of mercy, the Lord will let it be known publicly in hope they will finally break and have a spirit of repentance.

The power of cursing and blessing is really your choice, and I hope you can see it is a value to which Heaven responds.

The Currency
OF PRAYER

IN this chapter my goal is not to attempt to convince you to pray, but to show you what happens in the heavenly realm when you do pray. Also, in the hope that if you understand the processing of prayer and the attention it is given in the throne room of God, you will pray more intently and more often. Prayer is perhaps the most talked about topic in Christian circles—but the least used. We use the term *prayer* as a way of letting people know we are thinking about them. So why is prayer the simplest to do yet the least used when it comes to activating Heaven? I think if we understood our heavenly account and how much prayer is used in the deposit of our account, we would be more intentional in filling our depository.

John tells us in Revelation 5:8 (NKJV): *"Now when He had taken the scroll, the four living creatures and the twenty-four elders fell down before the Lamb, each having a harp, and golden bowls full of incense, which are the prayers of the saints."* Incense in Scripture represents the presence of God like a cloud. It also is seen as the arising of the voice of God's people to Him as prayer. Also the sweet aroma ascending is seen as the communion and fellowship between God and His saints. Prayer took on a more direct connection in the New Testament than the Old.

In the Old Covenant, the priesthood was the intermediator between God and humankind, primarily because of their rejection of God. When Moses led them to Mount Sinai, God manifested on the mountain with fire and quaking. The people, having never seen anything like that, told Moses he should go and talk to God for them. The Hebrews were content to stay distant from the presence of God. Moses, however, wanted more than the miracles he had witnessed through his hands. In Exodus 33, Moses asks to see God's glory, not just the manifestations or results of His presence being present. Moses wanted to enter God's essence we call glory. From that encounter, God set up the priesthood through Moses and his brother Aaron and particularly through the tribe of Levi. The Levitical priesthood was born. They were to represent the people to God and God to the people. Only a few designated prophets could speak or hear God's voice and words.

Jesus came to reconnect the people to God through His priesthood that came through the tribe of Judah, not Levi. Jesus broke the priestly mold allowing us to come directly to God through Him, the Son of God, not through a system that did not allow for communion and intimacy with our Father God. Covenant is huge for us to understand to pray effectively and with greater faith. I will share more about covenant later in this chapter.

John 16:23 (NKJV) says, *"And in that day you will ask Me nothing. Most assuredly, I say to you, whatever you ask the Father in My name He will give you."* The day Jesus was referring to was when He would return and sit at the right side of His Father. Prayer is now ratified by the blood of Jesus and His resurrection purchased our redemption, bringing us back into the plan of God before the fall of Adam. Before the glory departed from Adam and Eve, communication with God was very natural and normal. They were attracted to the sound of God walking or moving in the Garden of Eden, God's Headquarters on earth.

God's desire from the beginning was for His image in us, His creation, to communicate with Him so we could know His desires and plans. Jesus says in John 14:13-14 (NIV), *"And I will do whatever you ask in my name, so that the Father may be glorified in the Son. You may ask me for anything in my name, and I will do it."* Jesus makes it clear that He came to reveal the Father as He once stated to Philip, *"Anyone who has seen me has seen the Father"* (John 14:9 NIV).

Prayer is using the name of Jesus as the One who has access to the Father, and Jesus is willing to answer prayer so that the Father is glorified, meaning He magnifies the One who has the power and might to perform the answer to prayer. Using the name of Jesus is more than the ending of a prayer. *"Nor is there salvation in any other, for there is no other name under heaven given among men by which we must be saved"* (Acts 4:12 NKJV). The name of Jesus, who is the captain of the angelic host, is the name that activates everything in Heaven. *"Therefore God also has highly exalted Him and given Him the name, which is above every name, that at the name of Jesus every knee should bow, of those in heaven, and of those on earth, and of those under the earth"* (Philippians 2:9-10 NKJV).

In Jewish culture, a son came of age usually at the age of the age of thirteen. *Bar* in Hebrew means *son* or in some cases "from the house of." A *bar mitzvah* signified a son coming of age and he was then able to conduct business in the family name. When Jesus was baptized by John in the Jordan River, the heavens were opened and a Voice said, *"This is My beloved Son, in whom I am well pleased"* (Matthew 3:13-17 NKJV). This is similar to what a Jewish father would say over his son at a bar mitzvah. Jesus overcame through humanity on earth without sin and now intercedes for us as the only begotten Son of the Father who can conduct the business of Heaven and earth through His name.

Now after knowing this little bit of what is in a name, we should want to pray with more assurance that our prayers have significance. You have probably heard that nothing happens without prayer—now we know that without His name, prayer has no authority. We have heard the phrase, "Stop in the name of the law." There is truth to this in that a police officer only has authority when working under the covering of the laws and inside those parameters.

The Word of God, the Bible, tells us that if we ask anything in the name of Jesus, He will do it so His Father will be glorified. Many, though, take this out of the confines and Spirit of the Word. For example, if I should ask for something that is not the desire and plan of God for my life, He will not do it, as it would not glorify or reveal the purpose of God. Jesus did not command the stones to become bread when the devil was testing Him. Though He had the power and authority to do so, He didn't for two reasons: one, He would not yield to the tricks of the devil; two, He would not use His authority to fulfill His own desire.

MY HOUSE SHALL BE CALLED A HOUSE OF PRAYER

Matthew 21:13 tells us, *"And He said to them, 'It is written, "My house shall be called a house of prayer," but you have made it a "den of thieves."'"* When Jesus entered Jerusalem for the last time, known as His Triumphal Entry, riding on a donkey, the crowds shouted, *"Hosanna to the Son of David! Blessed is He who comes in the name of the Lord!"* (Matthew 21:1-9 NKJV). Jesus entered the temple and saw the crooked money changers cheating, people who were exchanging their currency to buy

sacrificial animals, and selling inferior animals for sacrifice. In this familiar passage, Jesus is quoting from Isaiah 56:7 as a promise that His house of prayer would be open to all nations, not only Jews.

At that time, the temple with its priestly rule and order was still in place. There is more to this verse than just the temple being the place to offer prayer. Hebrews 3:6 (NKJV) says, *"but Christ as a Son over His own house, whose house we are if we hold fast the confidence and the rejoicing of the hope firm to the end."* After the resurrection, the temple in Jerusalem was no longer the only temple of God. *We* became temples of God and houses of prayer. Jesus has driven out the sin and made us a place of prayer and worship. Anytime and anyplace you decide to pray, you have priestly access through Jesus the Author and Finisher of our faith. He is now the priest in charge of His house.

Hebrews 3:1 (NASB) as tells us, *"Therefore, holy brothers and sisters, partakers of a heavenly calling, consider the Apostle and High Priest of our confession: Jesus."* Our prayers confess Jesus as the One who presents our prayers to the Father in His name. It helps me to know that my prayers are not bouncing around the universe without landing at the right place. The name of Jesus is the zip code that ensures our prayers will reach the throne of grace to find help in time of our need.

HOLY SPIRIT PRAYER PARTNER

The Holy Spirit is our Prayer Partner when we allow Him to use the language that is beyond our ability, the language of Heaven. The Baptism in the Holy Spirt is crucial in our spiritual journey. Paul writes in Romans 8:26-27 (NKJV):

Likewise the Spirit also helps in our weaknesses. For we do not know what we should pray for as we ought, but the Spirit Himself makes intercession for us with groanings which cannot be uttered. Now He who searches the hearts knows what the mind of the Spirit is, because He makes intercession for the saints according to the will of God.

For a lot of people, their number-one reason for not praying is the struggle of knowing what to pray for and how to ask or what words to use about what they desire to see answered. The solution is to be aware that the Holy Spirit is present to help our inability to pray. He will even pray for a more effective prayer life. As the Scripture plainly says, He knows the *"mind of the Spirit"* and will make intercession according to the will of God. Being in partnership with the Holy Spirit takes the guesswork out of praying.

The Holy Spirit was present when creation was forged, and He was present when the Word of God was given to mankind. So, He is the best partner to have inside us praying. John 14:26 (NKJV) says, *"But the Helper, the Holy Spirit, whom the Father will send in My name, He will teach you all things, and bring to your remembrance all things that I said to you."* When Jesus returned to the Father and took His seat as the Intercessor for those in covenant with Him, He sent the Holy Spirit to not just be with us as Jesus was with the disciples, but now He has moved to inside us (Hebrews 9:24). Just think of it this way, in the New Covenant God moved from being inside a box called the Ark of the Covenant to living inside of us. We each are a temple with the Helper called the Holy Spirit living inside this temple. We need our minds to rethink time and space.

The normal, natural mindset is to look up and think light years away is Heaven, and God lives so far away our mind cannot fathom it. Here

is the rethink thought, by realizing God is not any farther away as my breath and if I believe He is that close, then perhaps praying doesn't seem so difficult and unbelievable. Romans 10:6-8 (NKJV) illuminates this truth:

> But the righteousness of faith speaks in this way, "Do not say in your heart, 'Who will ascend into heaven?' (that is, to bring Christ down from above) or 'Who will descend into the abyss?' (that is, to bring Christ up from the dead)." But what does it say? "The word is near you, in your mouth and in your heart" (that is, the word of faith which we preach.)

The apostle Paul received heavenly revelation more than most, and he described this divine connection that God is present through the Holy Spirit even in our mouth. So, we don't need to think of being separated by time and space and hope for a prayer to break through to get to God. The Word is present in us through faith.

If you are scrambling to know how to pray over a tough situation and are having difficulty finding the wording, stop and ask the Holy Spirit to help you, then trust Him to pray through you. He needs your cooperation to start the flow, but then He kicks into hyperdrive according to what God has already set aside for you. He is actually that close, and He is rooting for you to win the battle. He won't fight without you, but He certainly will join in and even take the lead in the charge.

He is also close enough to convict us of any sin that is hindering us from entering the place of victory. He knows how to prepare us to meet the Lord, since He is the seal upon our hearts unto the day of redemption.

COVENANT IS THE KEY TO EFFECTIVE PRAYER

The biggest discovery for me related to prayer and communing with the Lord was covenant. I think covenant and what it really means is one of the most overlooked themes of the New Testament. When we understand covenant, our faith and confidence to pray increases exponentially. First, we should know that God does nothing without covenant. Everything He has done and will do is because of covenant. There is a big difference between a contract and a covenant, at least in biblical terms. A contract is an agreement between two parties of equal ability to perform the promise or agreement. A promissory note would be like a mortgage on a house. With any agreement between people, things can happen and the contract may be broken.

As much as we put faith in a solidly worded contract, it's only as good as the two parties making the contract.

A covenant is different because God does not depend on us keeping our end of the agreement, and yet He continues to be faithful in His word to us. Our praying would be shaky if we knew that at any time God could break or rescind His promise to us. The first covenant made was a marriage covenant between Adam and his wife, Eve. The Hebrew word for *covenant* is *beriyth,* which means to cut. In this case, Adam's side was opened and a woman was formed from his bone, thus the well-known quote from Genesis 2:23 (NKJV), *"This is now bone of my bones and flesh of my flesh; she shall be called Woman, because she was taken out of Man."* Jesus made covenant with us when His side was pierced, thus the cut ratified our covenant as a type of bride taken from His side.

Adam showed us that man could not keep covenant, rather, he was a covenant breaker. Today over 50 percent of marriages end in divorce,

breaking covenant. When a covenant is broken, the strength that the two parties had together is broken and divided and the potential lost. The devil knows if he can divide us through a covenant-breaking spirit, we are weakened and ineffective against the gates of hell. God's solution was Jesus. His covenant could not depend upon mankind to fulfill.

We see the dynamic of this played out in Genesis 15 from where the premise of the currency of Heaven is found. In verse 5, God invites Abram to step outside his tent and look up and count the stars (more information is found in my book, *The Power of Imagination*). God wanted Abram to see for himself what his legacy and generations would look like, which was more than he could count. In verse 6, Abram believed God accounted it to him for righteousness. In verse 8, Abram asks the legitimate question, "How will I know that I will inherit it?" In verses 10-12, God gives him the assurance that what was promised would not be reversed or broken. He instructed Abram to prepare a sacrifice and the animals he was to use. He was to cut them in half placing each half opposite the other. When Abram had finished preparing the sacrifice and the sun was going down, a deep sleep fell upon him.

> *And it came to pass, when the sun went down and it was dark, that behold, there appeared a smoking oven and a burning torch that passed between those pieces. On the same day the Lord made a covenant with Abram...* (Genesis 15:17-18 NKJV).

When the two elements passed between the sacrifices, it was the Father and Son making covenant on behalf of Abram. Man showed he could not keep covenant, so God put Abram to sleep like He did Adam to cut covenant, only this time it would be a covenant that could not be

broken. I suggest to you, that Abram's Covenant is really a Covenant between the Father and the Son of God. The reason this is important is because Jesus the Son represents those who broke covenant and He has restored us to the Father's House.

When our prayers are answered, it is more about the Covenant of Jesus with His Father than our flawless living. Just as in Exodus 12 when the blood of a lamb was placed upon the doorposts, the angel of death passed over that house, the blood represented a covenant between God and His Son—His Son Jesus who became the Lamb slain, whose blood cries out in our defense.

There is another type of covenant used in the New Testament which is called the *diatheke*. This is like a couple purchasing a home of great value, and they have to borrow or make a loan or mortgage to buy this home. If the buyers are a credit risk and not able to secure the loan based on their credit history, they could invite a cosigner to sign with them. In this case the biblical term is the *diatheke* or cosigner. The *diatheke* is responsible for all the liability should the borrowers, enjoying the benefits of the home, not be able to pay the loan.

We can see how this fits perfectly as our Lord and Savior Jesus Christ. He took upon Himself all our sins and gave us eternal life abundantly without us having to pay the penalty of sin, which is death, eternal separation from God in eternal torment. Jeremiah 31:33 describes the covenant that God has brought to us through His Son. Jeremiah prophesies that the Covenant He will make will be written upon the heart and minds of the people, and we would be His people and He would become our God. Having a covenant heart not only is the guarantee of our relationship with God sealed by the Holy Spirit, but it helps us to pray in faith believing our Diatheke is listening and agreeing with our heart's cry.

STANDING ON HIS WORD, BACKED BY HIS COVENANT

When I first moved to Tyler to plant a church in 1980, I had a promise given to me the day I was driving a truck with all our earthly possessions to Tyler. Though I felt it was the Lord leading me to this new city, it still felt somewhat strange. I had never done anything to this level. Diane and I had two children at the time, and the thought of uprooting them and taking them 500 miles away from their grandparents was unsettling.

I was two hours away from our new destination and I couldn't stand it anymore—the gut wrenching I was feeling. I pulled the truck over to the side of the road when I was outside Dallas, Texas, and lay my head on the steering wheel, because I was close to turning around and going back to what was familiar. I had no family and not really any support system in Tyler. I softly said to the Lord what was in my heart and why I was feeling grief, as if I had lost a close family member. I really wasn't expecting to get a response from the Lord since I was basically just venting my feelings.

A couple of minutes later I heard deep inside my heart the Lord speaking to me. I know it was the Lord because it was different from what I was feeling, and He wasn't confirming my pity party. He said to me so sweetly that if would go and do what He was instructing me to do in Tyler, He would take care of my family and I would not lack for anything. Specifically He said, "I will be the Lord God who heals you and anyone in your family." I felt strength inside of my being again and was renewed to continue.

To think what I would have missed had I given in to my feelings and not heard the voice of the Lord makes me shudder. We had only been in Tyler a few months when Kristen, our youngest at the time, just one year

old, was suffering with an ear infection. Her mortal cries of pain were more than I could bear. I wished I could take her pain upon myself to give her relief.

We took her to see a pediatrician and he confirmed not only the infection, but it was acute, and antibiotics were not going to cure it. It was suggested she have surgery in the morning to have tubes inserted into both ears to drain the fluid that built up due to the infection. We set the surgery for early morning. At home, we went into her nursery and stood beside her bed and cried out to the Lord. The Holy Spirit reminded me of the promise the Lord made to me on the side of the road just a few months ago. I recited verbatim what I heard in my spirit that day. I quoted Numbers 23:19 (NKJV), *"God is not a man, that He should lie, nor a son of man, that He should repent. Has He said, and will He not do? Or has He spoken, and will He not make it good?"* I made a bold statement at the end of the prayer saying, "God, You told me if came to Tyler and obeyed You, You would heal my family. If I heard You wrong then, I should pack up and move back to my hometown."

The next morning, we arrived at the hospital and I handed Kristen to the surgical nurse with my heart breaking for my baby. The nurse said it would take a couple of hours for the procedure to do both ears. While we waited, I was thinking in my mind where I could go to rent a truck to pack our stuff and leave. For me, this was as much a test to know if I really heard God or not. I didn't want to be somewhere I was not absolutely sure I was supposed to be there with God's favor.

It was just a few minutes later when the same surgical nurse came over and asked if this was the same baby they had seen yesterday. I answered, "Yes, she is the only little girl I have." She turned around and went back into the surgical area. I was now really bothered as to what is going on and what had they done to her. Less than ten minutes later they brough Kristen out and handed her to me and said, "The pediatrician examined

her once more before doing any surgery and looking closely in both ears, he could not find any problem or abnormality."

I learned that day that God's word and covenant were not dependent on my strength—I had a *Diatheke* who kept the covenant promise of healing my family. Psalm 107:20 (NKJV) says, *"He sent His word and healed them."* The word that was given to me was the currency that I needed to see the miracle for my daughter. Prayer is not just asking for stuff, it is communicating with the Father, who really wants us to know Him and trust Him.

I encourage you to keep a prayer journal with dates and detailed descriptions of your communication with the Lord. It doesn't have to be only what you are asking for, but consider it similar to a thread of text messages, even writing what you feel the Lord saying to you, because the voice of the Holy Spirit is inside you. The Holy Spirit will share what He hears from your heavenly Father.

From time to time go back and read the dialogue between you and the Holy Spirit. This will help you to grow in hearing the voice of the Lord and to revisit things you are believing for. By reminding yourself of those things you have asked for and bringing them up in prayer again is like watering the seed sown.

Another good reason to go over past communications is to see if there are any conditions to what the Holy Spirit is saying, any area you may be lacking submission or obedience. Obedience changes things in your favor. I share more about this in the next chapter.

The Currency
OF AN OFFERING

T HE currency of Heaven is all about what the Bible teaches us that moves Heaven toward us. As already been stated in this writing, the angels respond to His Word and His Voice (Psalm 103:20). Also, heaven responds to offerings. Before I define more microscopically, let me state up front, I am not referring to monetary offerings alone for there are many different types of offerings. But at the core of each offering is the heart. Every offering reveals the heart.

> *Do not lay up for yourselves treasures on earth, where moth and rust destroy and where thieves break in and steal; but lay up for yourselves treasures in heaven, where neither moth nor rust destroys and where thieves do not break in and steal. For where your treasure is, there your heart will be also* (Matthew 6:19-21 NKJV).

The heart is the GPS of the soul.

Proverbs 4:23 (NKJV) says, *"Keep your heart with all diligence, for out of it spring the issues of life."* The word *issues* here is regarding the

path or direction a life would take. The reminder is that our heart, or in this case, the soul decides our thoughts and sets our path. The writer is cautioning us to guard our heart so we are not hardened and cannot appropriately know how to respond to God's promptings. Actions are the outward manifestation of what the heart or soul is all about.

Jesus was standing near the offering box in the temple and knew that a certain widow lady had given two mites which would be about 25 cents today (Mark 12:43-44 NIV). Jesus said of her:

> *Truly I tell you, this poor widow has put more into the treasury than all the others. They all gave out of their wealth; but she, out of her poverty, put in everything—all she had to live on.*

The point being, the issues of the heart are not about the *quantity*, but the *quality* of the devotion. The woman could have easily qualified to receive alms, or the offering designated for the poor; but instead, she gave out of her own need. She could have also justified her reasons for not giving and holding on to the meager amount she had. Yet her offering was designated and dedicated to God where her hope was. What moves Heaven into earth is the devotion of the heart, not how much we give to get any attention in Heaven. *"So let each one give as he purposes in his heart, not grudgingly or of necessity; for God loves a cheerful giver"* (2 Corinthians 9:7 NKJV). Not only is the offering an expression of the heart, it's the attitude in which it is offered that makes the difference.

Cheerful is the Greek word *hilaros,* from which we get the English word *hilarious. Hilarious* speaks of the readiness and looking forward to the offering, which is an act of worship. The rest of this verse explains another aspect to giving, which is to first purpose in our heart what we

will give. This implies some forethought in the giving process, not just a last-minute reaction. So this verse is boiled down to this, let us determine ahead of time what we will do or give and look forward to giving it. We could say then, the offering that gets God's attention is one that has been given forethought, and done so with joy.

From Heaven's point of view the value isn't the offering itself but the representation of the heart fully devoted in the process of giving. First Samuel 16:7 (NIV) is a perfect example of this:

> *But the Lord said to Samuel, "Do not consider his appearance or his height, for I have rejected him. The Lord does not look at the things people look at. People look at the outward appearance, but the Lord looks at the heart."*

When God was choosing a king for Israel, He told Samuel not to choose based on external appearances, because God looks at the heart. In order to understand what gets the attention of the heavenly and what makes deposits there, we must understand the perspective of Heaven.

Jesus gives us the model prayer in Matthew 6 for us to understand how to access His realm, by addressing God as Father and inviting His Kingdom to come and rule here on earth, but also in our hearts. Whoever governs our heart has our devotion and attention. Jesus also instructs in His prayer, *"Your will be done, on earth as it is in heaven."* Let us model our heart from the perspective of Heaven, not from whatever the trending pop culture is at the time. Psalm 50:21 (NKJV) makes this point without any ambiguity. God says, *"These things you have done, and I kept silent; you thought that I was altogether like you; but I will rebuke you and set them in order before your eyes."* I am thankful God is not like us or we may be able to get ahead of His plans and miss the preparation

we need. We need the Holy Spirit to guide us as to what is the offering or sacrifice required or needed to please the Lord. Though He is not like us in design, He has placed His likeness in us so that we might pursue Him and want to be in His presence.

THE OFFERING THAT GETS GOD'S ATTENTION

Genesis 4 is the account of Cain and Abel. We are not given too much detail in the beginning except it came time for an offering. Somehow, these two brothers understood they were to honor God by giving an offering. Abel is described as a keeper of sheep, and Cain is a tiller of the ground. We are given a contrast between the two: one is shepherd and the other is a farmer. At this point there is nothing better or worse between them. The time came when they were to present their offerings before the Lord; and in essence, they were presenting their hearts before the Lord too. In Genesis 4:3, Cain brings *an offering of the fruit of the ground.* The ground represents part of what was cursed when Adam and Eve fell away from God's paradise.

God had told the first family that no longer would the ground yield easily, only by their own sweat equity would it produce (Genesis 3:17). Cain brought an offering that he had to work for. The story continues stating that Abel also brought his offering, the firstborn of his flock (Genesis 4:4). The flock represents, obviously, a blood sacrifice. Now let's contrast the two offerings and in doing so we also contrast the two hearts. We are not given much more description of Cain, only that he brought his offering from the ground. The narration about Abel was that he brought the firstborn from his flock. I believe that Abel wasn't

the only one who knew what God wanted as a sacrifice. They both must have known the two requirements—the first and a blood sacrifice. Cain could have traded for a lamb sacrifice, but instead he gave what he wanted to give.

I know there are some assumptions here, but it is proven with other Scriptures later in this chapter. Genesis 4:4-5 (NKJV) says, *"Abel also brought of the firstborn of his flock and of their fat. And the Lord respected Abel and his offering, but He did not respect Cain and his offering. And Cain was very angry, and his countenance fell."* The word *regard* or *respect* in the Hebrew means "to catch the gaze, to be recognized or be accepted." Cain knew that God had greater acceptance of Abel's offering than his own.

Some believe that God consumed the sacrifice by fire, which would leave nothing to wonder about how God felt about the offering. In any case, Cain was aware of the distinction of Abel's offering. Cain took this jealousy out on Abel, or perhaps at God, and Abel was the recipient of his anger. God even warned Cain that his face revealed what was happening in his heart; and because of this attitude, sin awaited at his door. Cain's anger ramped up to the point of murdering Abel. God responds to Cain by saying, *"The voice of your brother's blood cries out to Me from the ground"* (Genesis 4:10 NKJV). The curse that came on Cain marked him as a fugitive and a wanderer from which the ground also would not be favorable to him as a farmer.

Presenting offerings to the Lord should never be a casual matter; we must consider the condition of our heart each time. Hebrews 11:4 (NKJV) tells us:

> *By faith Abel offered to God a more excellent sacrifice than Cain, through which he obtained witness that he was righteous,*

God testifying of his gifts; and through it he being dead still speaks.

And Hebrews 11:6 (NIV) says, *"And without faith it is impossible to please God, because anyone who comes to him must believe that he exists and that he rewards those who earnestly seek him."*

Another amazing view of the Hebrews passage is that God was testifying of Abel's gifts—and for six thousand years his offering is still speaking. Abel's offering testified that God existed by giving the best he had and showed his forethought of how God would view or consider his actions.

Contrarywise, nothing is mentioned of Cain having faith in connection with his offering. Without faith there is no regard for God, or perhaps this reveals his doubts. Two family strains are exposed here. Just as Cain's parents gave in to the doubts the serpent posed in the garden, Cain may have given in to his doubts too after God rejected his sacrifice. Whereas Abel showed the redemptive side of the family that God is who He says He is and thus his offering showed it. Abel's blood had a voice that spoke into Heaven. Cain's voice spoke of the fallen nature of Adam and Eve. The blood sacrifice from Abel was prophetically speaking of the receptiveness of God who would offer His own sacrifice and His own blood speaking over all mankind.

THE OFFERING THAT DESTROYED OUR ENEMY

John 3:16 (NKJV) declares, *"God so loved the world that He gave His only begotten Son, that whoever believes in Him should not perish but have*

everlasting life." This crown text of the Bible is all about an offering. God set the precedent for giving, because through His giving the work of the devil was destroyed. Just think about it. It was an offering that broke the yoke of slavery from our necks. God did not send an angel or some other sacrifice, He sent His Son down to earth as His own offering. The devil certainly didn't see that one coming, or he would have never crucified the only begotten Son of the Father (1 Corinthians 2:8).

God gave His best for us; He did not spare anything to redeem us from the curse that Adam's disobedience brought upon the world. Giving totally disarms the devil, which is the opposite of his nature. God's nature is to give; but more than just give, His nature is to give the best, which represents how He feels about us.

First John 3:8 (NIV) says, *"The one who does what is sinful is of the devil, because the devil has been sinning from the beginning. The reason the Son of God appeared was to destroy the devil's work."* Abel's offering was a prophetic image of the New Covenant that was ratified through an offering.

And Matthew 5:23-24 (NIV) confirms what our intentions for giving must be: *"Therefore if you bring your gift to the altar, and there remember that your brother has something against you, leave your gift there before the altar and go your way. First be reconciled to your brother, and then come and offer your gift."* Again, Jesus makes the point that the offering is received or rejected based upon the heart, showing the heart is more important than the offering itself. We cannot give our way out of the condition of a hard heart. The heart condition either validates or rejects everything we do unto the Lord.

The good news is that we can correct the issues of the heart and then the offering will be accepted, and favor will be restored. Reconciliation is the first order before the offering. Relationships between one

another is an issue of the heart that interrupts the power of the offering. There are times when a person refuses to accept forgiveness, but you are free because you tried to reconcile—so your heart is no longer under condemnation.

Jesus asks the question in Matthew 23:19 (NIV), *"Which is greater: the gift, or the altar that makes the gift sacred?"* The gift has importance; but the altar, the platform, from which the gift is offered either sanctifies the offering or pollutes the offering. Guarding the heart is a great admonishment so that we are not presenting offerings that are not accepted into our account.

THE QUESTION POSED TO
ME BY THE LORD

I am surprised at times by questions that I know are posed to me by the Lord. The questions are so poignant that I know there is no way it is my own imagination. One day while driving to a meeting where I was scheduled to speak, I heard the Lord ask me, "Kerry, do you think you can be bound in Heaven and thus be bound on earth?" One thing for sure is that if the Lord is asking the question, I must not have the right answer. I said out loud since I was in my truck alone, "I know that is the verse you gave to Peter in Matthew 16 that gives us authority to bind what is already bound in Heaven and loose on earth what is already loosed in Heaven."

I heard Him say, "Yes, that is true, but can a person be bound in Heaven though they themselves are binding the enemy on earth?" I finally conceded, "Only You know the answer." I wasn't sure where the conversation was taking me. Then I felt the Holy Spirt help me with

the answer: If I don't forgive others on earth, I am bound in Heaven—because if I don't forgive, I cannot be forgiven. The simplicity of that statement hit me between the eyes. For the next few miles, I meditated on what was told me.

I asked the Holy Spirit to search me (Psalm 139:23-24) and see if there was anything in me that would cause me to be bound in Heaven. The thought that I was shadowboxing with no authority on earth to battle the enemy was shocking. I knew this revelation was not just for me to share when I spoke at the meeting, but the Lord was doing business with my heart. I knew there had to be something specific that would pollute the altar of my heart, and I just couldn't randomly repent for something I had not been made mindful of.

Before the evening concluded, the Holy Spirit brought to my mind a betrayal that had happened many years before. I thought I had released the person, but then I would justify my resistance every time the person's name was brought up in casual conversation. I knew for the Holy Spirit to target this particular time of pain was because it was holding me back from entering the next level of authority. I needed desperately to realize this unforgiveness so I would not be on pause anymore. I asked the Holy Spirit to help me to release the person without any punitive thought in my heart.

For the first time I could see the person who pained me in a different light. I saw the turmoil in the person's life, so I was able to have empathy and understanding of the actions done toward me. I was able to bless the individual sincerely and ask forgiveness, and I felt the release in my heart. Today I can see the person and even talk to them without feeling defensive or feeling any need to impress. Just like the bank lets us know when our account is overdrawn, so the Holy Spirit lets us know our assets are frozen until we take care of what is binding us in Heaven.

OBEDIENCE IS BETTER THAN SACRIFICE

First Samuel 15:22 (NKJV) admonishes us:

> *Samuel said, "Has the Lord as great delight in burnt offerings and sacrifices, as in obeying the voice of the Lord? Behold, to obey is better than sacrifice, and to heed than the fat of rams. For rebellion is as the sin of witchcraft, and stubbornness is as iniquity and idolatry. Because you have rejected the word of the Lord, He also has rejected you from being king."*

The back story to this Scripture passage is King Saul was instructed by God to destroy everything of the Amalekites. When Samuel the prophet arrived to inspect the mission, he heard the animals and sees Agag, the king of Amalek. When Samuel asked why everything wasn't destroyed as God demanded, Saul made excuses. He blamed the people who took the best of the animals, but he said he destroyed everything else. Saul said he was keeping some good animals to make a sacrifice to the Lord. Samuel puts sacrifice into perspective, by saying, *"Has the Lord as great delight in sacrifices as in obeying the voice of the Lord?"*

The answer is important, because God views obedience more important than any sacrifice or offering. The reason is consistent with all I have shared in this chapter, which is *obedience is an expression of the heart.* Sacrifices are an outward expression, but the internal altar of the heart decides whether the offering is acceptable.

The rest of Saul's story is sad; because of his disobedience or partial obedience, it cost him his position as king. Though Saul continued to blame the people by saying he feared the people and obeyed their voice, not only was he disobedient to God but he also confessed that he feared

people more than he feared God. The quickest way to lose authority with God is to disobey and not fear Him.

Case in point, see Acts 5:3-4 (NKJV):

> *Peter said, "Ananias, why has Satan filled your heart to lie to the Holy Spirit and keep back part of the price of the land for yourself? While it remained, was it not your own? And after it was sold, was it not in your own control? Why have you conceived this thing in your heart? You have not lied to men but to God."*

During this time in the early church there was great power demonstrated by the apostles, giving witness to the resurrection, and great grace was upon the people (Acts 3:33). There was such a spirit of giving that believers were selling land and houses and bringing the proceeds to the apostles to be distributed to the poor. It was not unusual for large sums of money to be brought for distribution.

A couple named Ananias and his wife Sapphira sold a possession and brought it to the disciples for distribution. They conspired together to keep back a portion of themselves. There was nothing required of them to give all of it, but they led the apostles to believe they had given it all. Peter said to them, *"Why has Satan filled your heart to lie to the Holy Spirit. You have not lied to men but to God."* At separate times, each fell down dead.

Again, the offering is secondary to what is going on in the heart. In this case the couple lied by appearing to be something they were not. They wanted people to see them as generous and part of what God was doing. It would have been better to offer nothing than a partial amount

with deception. Obedience and truth are key to giving an acceptable offering.

> *Therefore, when you do a charitable deed, do not sound a trumpet before you as the hypocrites do in the synagogues and in the streets, that they may have glory from men. Assuredly, I say to you, they have their reward. But when you do a charitable deed, do not let your left hand know what your right hand is doing, that your charitable deed may be in secret; and your Father who sees in secret will Himself reward you openly* (Matthew 6:2-4 NKJV).

Genesis 22:1 God tested Abraham with offering his son Isaac. When God tests something it is for the purpose of inspection of the heart to see if the one being tested is ready for the next level or weight of glory. Two words are used for *testing*. The first one is *temptation*, used to describe when a person is pulled by something of his or her own carnal nature. This type of temptation is described in James 1:13-14. The other word for *test* is used to test for quality of construction, to determine structural strength, to build upon, as described by the parable in Matthew 7:24-27. The house that was prepared properly withstood the test.

Perhaps the test for Abraham was one of prioritized devotion. By offering his son, he was to show that the gift from God, a son, had not taken the place of the Giver of the gift, which in this case was God. Had the gift of God become more important than the Giver of the gift? Abraham passed the test.

Years ago, someone in my church approached me who wanted prayer concerning a job opportunity. He explained this would be his dream job, working for the state overseeing parks. Then he gave this caveat,

there were other senior people in line for the job. We both agreed God could do a miracle and even create a new position. A few weeks later he stopped me and excitedly shared how he got the job. He began by saying, "You won't believe what it took for me to get this job."

The narrative was somewhat bizarre, one man had died unexpectedly, another man retired, and the third man was transferred to a different district. We both agreed this was an unusual miracle and praised the Lord for it. Several weeks passed and I had not seen this man or his family, so I decided to call to see how they were adjusting to the new job plus the substantial raise in salary. He was happy to hear from me, and told me that his schedule now prevented him from attending church due to travel and the long hours and the pressure of deadlines. He was still excited about the job and made a few promises to get back into fellowship with the church family. That was the last time I ever spoke to him or saw him. I'm not sure how things ended up for him, but I couldn't help feeling that the gift had become more important than the One who provided it.

Perhaps this next verse will shed some understanding why God had accounted to Abraham righteousness. Genesis 22:5: *"Abraham said to his young men, 'Stay here with the donkey; the lad and I will go yonder and worship, and we will come back to you.'"* Abraham had such faith in God that he knew if he sacrificed his son, God was able to raise him up again. Here is his faith statement to the servants, *"the lad and I are going to worship, and **we** will return to you."* Abraham saw the test as an act of worship, and they would return.

The rest of the story continues to be faith building when Abraham's son Isaac says, *"The fire and wood are here, but where is the lamb for the burnt offering?"* (Genesis 22:7-8 NIV). Abraham's answered is filled with faith saying, *"My son, God will provide* [Jehovah Jireh] *for Himself the lamb for a burnt offering"* (Genesis 22:8 NIV). Notice Abraham

didn't say it would be a sacrifice for himself or Isaac—it was a sacrifice for the Lord Himself.

The whole time Abraham was moving in obedience, and he had an eye open for the provisional lamb of God. The test proved Abraham would not withhold the very best from God. Since God is omniscient, knowing everything, this test was to show Abraham his own heart and the strength of his faith. Ultimately, in verse 13, God provided a ram caught in a thicket at the right time and perfectly placed. This is a powerful picture of God's plan of redemption for the whole world. God did not withhold His own Son, showing His perfect love.

WHEN DOES AN OFFERING BECOME A WEAPON?

Judges 6 reveals a powerful story that sends a clear message to every generation. This was in a time when Israel did evil in the sight of the Lord. It's important to underscore the opening verse to this story (Judges 6:1), that the evil was how God looked at it; it was not based upon the trend of popular culture at that time. What seems to be normal could be considered evil in the sight of the Lord. Israel had become accustomed to the idolatry and perversion of the day. The judgment lasted seven years, administered by the Midianites. Judges 6:3 describes Israel's desperation; whenever Israel had sown seeds, the enemy would wait for the time of harvest and raid the fruit of their labor. The people of Israel were hiding in caves and dens trying to exist while living in poverty and fear of the next attack.

Judges 6:11 tells of the beginning of change, when God sent an angel to enlist Gideon to be the deliverer of the people. It was time for their judgment to change into victory. Gideon asks:

> *"O my lord, if the Lord is with us, why then has all this happened to us? And where are all His miracles which our fathers told us about, saying, 'Did not the Lord bring us up from Egypt?' But now the Lord has forsaken us and delivered us into the hands of the Midianites." Then the Lord turned to him and said, "Go in this might of yours, and you shall save Israel from the hand of the Midianites. Have I not sent you?"* (Judges 6:13-14 NKJV)

I think it's interesting the angel did not answer Gideon's "why" question about the misfortune that happened to them. The angel would only tell him the "what," not the "why." The mission at hand is not to look back and feel pity, it's time to go forward and deliver Israel from Midian.

Continuing the same conversation, Gideon says, *"Please do not go away until I come back and bring my offering and set it before you.' And the Lord said, 'I will wait until you return'"* (Judges 6:18 NIV). Gideon still wasn't sure if the angel of God was for real or if perhaps he was imagining something.

The test was for the angel to remain until Gideon could bring him an offering. Since there were no fast-food places for goats and bread, it took several hours to prepare. Gideon left and prepared a young goat and unleavened bread and some broth and brought it to the angel as an offering.

Judges 6:21 tells us: *"Then the Angel of the Lord put out the end of the staff that was in His hand and touched the meat and the unleavened bread; and fire rose out of the rock and consumed the meat and the unleavened bread. And the Angel of the Lord departed out of his sight. Now Gideon perceived that He was the Angel of the Lord."*

Gideon, now convinced that the angel is real, is permitted to go and spy on the Midian camp. Gideon goes down to the Midian camp and overhears what two Midianites are saying. One man was telling a dream to his friend:

> *Gideon arrived just as a man was telling a friend his dream. "I had a dream," he was saying. "A round loaf of barley bread came tumbling into the Midianite camp. It struck the tent with such force that the tent overturned and collapsed." His friend responded, "This can be nothing other than the sword of Gideon son of Joash, the Israelite. God has given the Midianites and the whole camp into his hands"* (Judges 9-14 NIV).

Here is the kicker to this story, Gideon's offering became the weapon God used to defeat the enemy. After the interpretation of the dream by the Midianite friend, Gideon's faith greatly increased, and he obeyed God and Midian was slain. The takeaway message is that God can use the obedience of an offering to change defeat into victory.

The apostle Paul tells us in Romans 12:1 (NIV): *"Therefore, I urge you, brothers and sisters, in view of God's mercy, to offer your bodies as a living sacrifice, holy and pleasing to God—this is your true and proper worship."* Not only are there particular offerings that you are impressed by the Holy Spirit to offer, but the one offering that is absolutely required before anything else is yourself. You are the offering that catches the

gaze of Heaven. As you worship, you are doing more than singing songs. When your heart is the altar and the altar is pure, your sincere devotion rises to the heavens as a sweet-smelling incense.

When David had numbered the people who were eligible to be warriors, this angered the Lord because David was not trusting God to win victories—he was trusting in the armament that he commanded. A plague was released upon the people and David went to the threshing floor of a man named Araunah. When the man saw King David and knew he was there to make a sacrificial offering to the Lord, he offered to furnish everything for the King. David, understanding the offering needed to come from him, said, *"No, I insist on paying you for it. I will not sacrifice to the Lord my God burnt offerings that cost me nothing..."* (2 Samuel 24:24 NIV). An offering that costs us nothing is only an entitlement. The offering that has our heart in it has the value God is looking for. We cannot hire someone to worship for us, it must be our heart with our cost.

Galatians 2:20 (KJV) says, *"I am crucified with Christ: nevertheless I live; yet not I, but Christ liveth in me: and the life which I now live in the flesh I live by the faith of the Son of God, who loved me, and gave himself for me."* The greatest sacrifice that ever will be is the cross—and that is why we are to be crucified with Him, letting all our old sin nature and habits die there and only His life to be resurrected in us.

The Currency
OF LOVE

I N this last chapter, it is fitting to highlight love as a currency that Heaven responds to. In this chapter, my expectations are that what you know about love from Heaven's perspective will take on a whole new in-depth understanding. With this new understanding, you will have imparted to you a new sense of power and authority from the Lord. Not only does the Holy Spirit and the angels respond to the Word of God they also are motivated by love. Allow me to begin with a few basic definitions that most are aware of to establish a foundation for the principle of love.

Though the Bible uses the word *love* more than 300 times, especially in the New Testament, most of the uses refer to love as *agape.* There are four uses of the word *love,* and each mean very different things depending on who is speaking and the context in which it is used.

We use the word *love* in many different ways, mainly to describe something we like or desire— anywhere from food to our favorite place to visit. This common use is *phileo,* meaning a feeling or sentiment about a friend or something you have a level of acquaintance. *Phileo* also means

a brotherly connection. For example, the city of Philadelphia is called the "City of Brotherly Love."

The next is *storge,* which is used in relationship to family, those who are in your bloodline. This a familial-type relationship that separates you from all others outside of your *storge.* The third type of love is *eros,* which is easy to connect with the term *erotic,* describing something of a sexual nature.

The love that best describes Heaven's design for this word is *agape.* Most will say this simply means unconditional love, which is true, but it has much more depth, which we will explore. Saying that *agape* is only unconditional love is like saying grace is only the unmerited favor of God. Both statements are the elementary sides of their meanings. However, in the revelation of the fullness of *agape,* lies a level of power and authority that most miss because they settle for surface meanings.

The very nature of God is love. First John 4:7-8 (NKJV) says, *"Beloved, let us love one another, for love is of God; and everyone who loves is born of God and knows God. He who does not love does not know God, for God is love."* Love is not an adjective about God, but Love is God.

Agape love is both a noun and a verb. God is love and what He does is from the basis and divine nature of who He is. We cannot separate God's love from what He does—even His judgment has love as the basis of His actions. Since agape love is not about an emotion or selfish stimulation, God's actions are based on His perspective, which is love. John 3:16 exemplifies how God so loved the world that His actions of placing His only Son as the scapegoat was not based on feelings or sentiment, but justice. To natural parents, it makes no sense to place our child in a harmful or destructive position. So we can see from this agape love is not a natural or a human instinct. Agape love is supernatural at its core.

With this perspective in mind, let's dive into a richer understanding of agape love. Agape love is the filter, or the way God views creation. Though His love is charitable, it's also righteousness, peace, and joy.

Ephesians 3:19-20 (NKJV) says, *"to know the love of Christ which passes knowledge; that you may be filled with all the fullness of God. Now to Him who is able to do exceedingly abundantly above all that we ask or think, according to the power that works in us."* The context of this passage has to do with knowing the love of Christ that leads us to the fullness of God. The exciting part of this verse is He is able to do things beyond what we can think of to the extent of the power that is working in us. There is no guessing here as to the fullness of the power that is to be at work in us, which is His love fully overtaking every part of our being.

I am certainly not at the point of being fully engulfed by His love. Notice the exceedingly and abundantly is not related to a particular gifting but divinely connected to His love. *Fullness* is the Greek word *pleroo,* which means to have no voids, to completely fill every nook and cranny. That is when the power of love spills over into the supernatural. Because of our humanity and living in a fallen world, this seems like an impossibility, and it is, when we to try to do it on our own. Our human instinct is to look for a formula or creative steps to get to this level of baptism.

"Now hope does not disappoint, because the love of God has been poured out in our hearts by the Holy Spirit who was given to us" (Romans 5:5 NKJV). Jesus knew we were not capable of such undertaking as being filled with His love by our own initiative, so He gave us the Holy Spirit to tutor us in all things that are from Jesus, and Jesus wants us to know the Father who is love (John 16:15).

THE MANTLE OF LOVE

Colossians 3:14-15 says, *"But above all these things put on love, which is the bond of perfection. And let the peace of God rule in your hearts, to which also you were called in one body, and be thankful."* The phrase "put on" is interesting in light of what agape love is. It tells me that agape love first off is a choice I have—to put on or not to put on. Once the choice is made in the sincerity of heart, the Holy Spirit starts the work of fashioning us to be outfitted, like a blacksmith would tailor-make a suit of armor. This verse includes the idea of perfect bonding or the bond of perfection. *Perfection* is the Greek word *telios*, meaning complete, nothing left to do or finish. The finished work of the cross certainly has love as the basis for offering one's life for another (John 15:13).

With this mantle of love in place, the next exhortation is to let the peace of God rule or take over the governing of the life of whomever wears His mantle of love. First John 3:1 (NKJV): *"Behold what manner of love the Father has bestowed on us, that we should be called children of God! Therefore, the world does not know us, because it did not know Him."* The message here using the term *bestowed* sounds very much like someone being knighted and conferring upon them a title of nobility. The love of God places upon us a garment of praise that identifies us as being under His domain to serve. Someone can serve without love, but no one can love without serving. Again, the imagery of being mantled or covered with an identity of His Kingdom carries with it protection from the evil one who would attempt to strip us of our identity, which has become the markings of the God who loves us.

There is always testing to see if we are walking in our identity of love. One of those moorings or tests is John 14:15, *"If you love Me, keep My commandments."* And Jude 1:21 (NKJV): *"Keep yourselves in the love of*

God, looking for the mercy of our Lord Jesus Christ unto eternal life." The guidance of the Holy Spirit is present to inspect our mantle of love. In Matthew 22, Jesus is sharing a parable about the Kingdom of God and likens it to a king who prepared a wedding feast. The original guests did not come, so he sent out more servants to invite whoever would come, which is a picture of the Gentiles being grafted into the vine.

When the king looked over the wedding feast, he noticed one who did not have on the traditional wedding garment. When asked why he was not wearing the wedding garment, the man was speechless. The king then ordered the servants to bind this man hand and foot and cast him out of the wedding party, relating to outer darkness and separation from God. This seems strange to our Western culture of today, especially as the guest was invited. The parable is very powerful when we understand the message through the Middle Eastern mindset. Every guest was met at the door and given a wedding garment to be placed over the attire they were wearing when then arrived.

No matter how noble they dressed or how poorly they were dressed, everyone was to be covered with the king's "mantle." The wedding garment usually had the crest of the king, which spoke of all the king's domain and victories. For the man to refuse to wear the garment and identify with the king was considered rebellion and disrespect to the king. In essence, the man wanted all the festivity and food that the king was providing at such a lavish wedding feast, but he did not want the covering of the king. His statement of independence spoke loudly among the crowd.

Without the love of God, we stand out from the crowd and become prey for the enemy to pick up on our rebellion and carry us off into darkness. Matthew 6:24 (NIV): *"No one can serve two masters. Either you will hate the one and love the other, or you will be devoted to the one and despise the other. You cannot serve both God and money."*

THE GIFT OF LOVE

Paul exhorts us concerning spiritual gifts in his letter to the Corinthian church. In 1 Corinthians 12, which is usually thought of as the Gifts of the Spirit chapter, he uses the analogy of the body to say we need all the parts of the body just as we need all the gifts in use for the good of the body of Christ. Then in 1 Corinthians chapter 14, the apostle Paul is teaching on prophecy and speaking in tongues. Right in the middle of these two chapters about various gifts is 1 Corinthians 13, commonly called the Love chapter. Originally the Scriptures were written without chapters and verses but as one continual thought as letters of instruction to the churches in various cities, hence the naming of the letters after where they were sent.

My reason for pointing this out is to show that the flow of thought concerning spiritual gifts were connected to the understanding that love was the gift that caused all the other gifts to function. Chapter 13 begins with the caution of not operating in gifts such as tongues if you don't do it in love. Without love, it is nothing more than a noisy clanging of brass cymbals. This description is a great image of how Heaven views us functioning in gifts of prophecy or in great faith and having gifts of knowledge—but without love, we are nothing but noise. However, when love is the lens used to look at giftings and the motivation for administering these gifts, love currency is deposited. In 1 Corinthians 13:4-7 the fruit of love is described as being patient, without envy, not boasting, and not proud or puffed up.

Love is also kind, not rude, not easily provoked, and thinks of no evil. Galatians 5:22 lists love as the first of the fruit of the Spirit. The word *fruit* means it's the result of something coming to fullness.

One of the questions on a test in my agriculture class was, "What is the difference between fruit and a vegetable?" I was glad I studied

the textbook. The correct answer is that fruit has the seed inside itself. Tomatoes are easily thought of as a vegetable, but really is classed as fruit. My point is, for something to be classed as fruit, it began with seed inside itself. The Word of God is called "seed," which is also translated as *sperma,* with the understanding that it will reproduce after its own kind, according to Genesis 1:1. When God told Adam and his wife to be fruitful and multiply, that increase came about by planting seed.

The same principle is applicable here with love. When love is sown, it reproduces the same fruit, and it then empowers the other gifts of manifestation to function. First Corinthians13:8-13 (NKJV) reveals more depth to what love is. Where there are prophecies they will fail, in eternity tongues will cease, and the last verse of this important love chapter says, *"And now abide faith, hope, love, these three; but the greatest of these is love."* First Corinthians 14:1 (NKJV) opens with, *"Pursue love, and desire spiritual gifts."* The strongest of the two admonitions is to pursue love, which is stronger than to desire spiritual gifts. If the desire for gifts outrun the pursuit of love, then we have a recipe for wreckage.

Recently I was asked the question by a group of hungry young leaders, "What can we do to increase the anointing in our ministries?" I realized they wanted me to enlarge on using three steps and five keys to get a greater anointing. My answer was simple and certainly less complicated than a large to-do list of steps. I said, "Make more room for the Holy Spirit and less room for selfishness. When love is the basis for ministry, not love for the ministry, anointing or divine enablement just happens. Since God is love and the anointing is God filling up the empty places, then anointing is present."

Anointing, like love, is not an emotion or feeling; although when love is present and His empowerment is being manifested, there certainly is cause for rejoicing and emotional feelings. John 13:34-35 (NKJV) says,

"A new commandment I give to you, that you love one another; as I have loved you, that you also love one another. By this all will know that you are My disciples, if you have love for one another." One of the signs of someone following Jesus is the interaction between followers. If there is competition or selfish ambition, then love has yet to find its perfect work. Nothing hinders the flow of the Holy Spirit more than when the works of flesh compete for position and notoriety.

PERFECT LOVE CASTS OUT FEAR

First John 4:17-18 (NKJV) tells us:

> *Love has been perfected among us in this: that we may have boldness in the day of judgment; because as He is, so are we in this world. There is no fear in love; but perfect love casts out fear, because fear involves torment. But he who fears has not been made perfect in love.*

John the beloved had an intimate understanding of what agape love consists of. He makes it clear that fear and agape cannot coexist in the same person at the same time. Love is a force that darkness cannot overpower. Love is not mere words of sentiment, it is the very nature of God Himself. Since God is Spirit, then agape love is also Spirit.

John aptly says fear involves torment. God's love is the anthesis of fear. Fear tries to fill up the void, and love dispels the fear. The key is, when fear tries to raise its tormenting head, all you need to do is turn your affection upon the Lord and allow love to flood your mind. Perfect love means it is complete, lacking nothing; it also means love is finished,

it has the last word if we allow it to become bigger than the fear. Whatever we magnify, we give power to it.

Psalm 34:3 (NKJV) says, *"Magnify the Lord with me, and let us exalt His name together."* *Magnify* means to enlarge, so let glory and praise overshadow the problem of fear. But many magnify the problem; and the more we fear it and discuss the size of the problem, the more power we give to the fear. To shrink the problem, we must exalt the solution, which is the love of God.

Isaiah 59:19 (NKJV) tells us, *"...When the enemy comes in like a flood, the Spirit of the Lord will lift a standard against him."* It's important to note that the enemy is not in charge of the flood. The enemy comes in, but it is the Lord who raises the standard against him. Likewise, Psalm 29:10 (NKJV) says, *"The Lord sat enthroned at the Flood...."* The love of God comes in like the flood to overwhelm the fear of the enemy.

So the question now is, what is the distinction between agape love and perfect agape love? John answers this for us in 1 John 2:4-5 (NIV), *"Whoever says, 'I know Him,' but does not do what he commands is a liar, and the truth is not in that person. But if anyone obeys his word, love for God is truly made complete in them. This is how we know we are in him."* Perfect love, remember, is not lacking—it is complete. John is saying to keep His Word, meaning live out the Word in daily life, don't just memorize the Word. Those who keep it are perfected in the agape love of God.

VIOLENCE OF THE KINGDOM

Matthew 11:12 (NKJV): *"And from the days of John the Baptist until now the kingdom of heaven suffers violence, and the violent take it by force."*

In the previous verses in Matthew 11, Jesus is commending John the Baptist by saying there is none greater than John, yet he who is least in the Kingdom of Heaven is greater than John. The word *violence* is easily misunderstood in this verse. Some think it is about being exuberant, but its way more than that. The word *violence* in the Greek is *biadzo*, meaning to crowd out and leave no room for anything else. Let's put it in context with the Kingdom of God.

When the Kingdom of God was established by the resurrection of Christ, the enemy was crowded out along with fear—sin no longer could hold us in slavery. The New King Jesus pushed out the old master of darkness, and everyone who enters will do the exploits of the King. John the Baptist's message prepared the way for the Lord. Jesus is the transition from the Old Covenant into the New Covenant, which opened the door to the Kingdom of God.

John the Baptist came preaching about the Kingdom of God; however, everyone who enters the Kingdom of God is greater than the one who preached about it. Jesus defines to some degree what the Kingdom of God is all about. Luke 11:20 (NKJV): *"But if I cast out demons with the finger of God, surely the kingdom of God has come upon you."* Jesus unveiled the Kingdom of God and is the demonstration of the power and authority of the King.

The dominion of the King is the Kingdom and all He rules over. Romans 14:17 (NKJV) says, *"for the kingdom of God is not eating and drinking, but righteousness and peace and joy in the Holy Spirit."* The very nature of the Kingdom of God carries the markings of the King of righteousness, peace, and joy. All three of these at some time describe Jesus the King of glory. Now we can add the layer of perfected love to the attributes of the Kingdom of God and realize the truth in Romans 8:31 (NKJV): *"What then shall we say to these things? If God is for us, who can be against us?"*

WHAT GOD HATES

Proverbs 6:16-19 (NIV) clearly states what God hates:

> *There are six things the Lord hates, seven that are detestable to him: haughty eyes, a lying tongue, hands that shed innocent blood, a heart that devises wicked schemes, feet that are quick to rush into evil, a false witness who pours out lies and a person who stirs up conflict in the community.*

Not only is it of importance to know God is love, we should also know what God hates. The Hebrew word for *hate* is *sane,* and comes from two pictures that the language uses for root words creating their meanings. In this case, the two pictures-letters are a thorn and a seed—depicted as a seed of a plant with barbs or thorns. Thus, hate means to avoid or turn away from and have no interaction.

In Middle Eastern life at the time of Jesus, they used barbed plants to build fences for protection or to set a boundary. In the context of what God hates, this could very well mean that He will not interact with these people and will instead avoid them. In the case with Cain and his offering, Genesis 4 says, that God had no regard of Cain's offering. And Romans 9:13 (NKJV) says, *"As it is written, 'Jacob I have loved, but Esau I have hated.'"* Three places in Scripture refer to God hating Esau but loving Jacob, so the point concerning these two brothers came down to God choosing. Esau obviously did not value his birthright enough to keep it and was willing to sell it to Jacob for a bowl of soup. God's plan for the nation of Israel came through Jacob; though Jacob was a deceiver, God's plan was not altered.

We see later in the lives of these two brothers, in their reconciliation, Esau also prospered though he lost the blessing of the firstborn. So we see here the idea that hate seemed to mean to avoid or pass by without regard. We can see how powerful God's love is, if His hate disregards, then how much more His love regards us by placing His mantle upon us, whereby we gain favor and blessing.

WHAT GOD LOVES

Paul states emphatically in 2 Corinthians 9:7 (NIV) what God loves:

> *Each of you should give what you have decided in your heart to give, not reluctantly or under compulsion, for God loves a cheerful giver.*

Cheerful in this context means hilarious in response to giving. A cheerful giver is someone who enjoys giving and is not doing so with resentment. If we are thinking to ourselves, *I could really use that money or gift myself more than the church,* we are not cheerful givers, we're obligated givers. God so loved that He gave to the world the best representation of Himself— His Son.

Love represents the condition of the heart. The size or the amount is not as important as the attitude in which we give—that is the revealing part. God has regard for those who cheerfully give.

Psalm 87:2 (NKJV) tells us that God loves worship and worshipers: *"The Lord loves the gates of Zion more than all the dwellings of Jacob."* Zion is a great symbol for worship. Zion is where Solomon's temple was built, which is known for its magnificence and importance in worship.

God loves worshipers. When time ceases on this earth many things will stop. There will be no need for preaching in Heaven and no need for calendars or clocks since time will cease as well.

We know for sure that love is eternal and will fill all of heaven. Worship will continue in Heaven. We should know what God loves will carry over into eternity. Loving what God loves will be deposited into our account in Heaven. God loves the poor and those who give mercy to the poor without judgment have a place with the Lord.

THE LOVE OF THE FATHER

Proverbs 3:12 (NKJV): *"For whom the Lord loves He corrects, just as a father the son in whom he delights."* In this verse we can see the depth of a father's heart. A father who loves will correct and discipline his child, not for his own anger or pleasure, but because he has vision for his child's potential. If children are left to their own ways and devices, they are without direction and can become wanderers, growing up as people who will always be wanton, looking for entitlements.

This present generation is facing generational identity issues. Most of the violence we see in the cities is largely due to living in a fatherless generation. By the term *fatherless* I am referring to fathers who abandon their children due to their own selfishness without bonding to those of their own flesh and blood. It's also possible to have a father living in the house, yet his heart is far from the family, possibly because the stress of making a living is overwhelming.

Another type of fatherlessness is someone who has provided well for the family but cannot bring himself to correct his children, not wanting them to be upset with him. In all these scenarios, the love of a father is

missing. Love of a father is not what the father can buy for the family. A father's role is like none other—he can provide for his children the affirmation of their identity as a person, even up to their sexuality, confirming that God has blessed them with who they are. Hebrews 12:8 (NIV) tells us: *"If you are not disciplined—and everyone undergoes discipline—then you are not legitimate, not true sons and daughters at all."*

Here is an interesting point. I have been writing about who God is in terms of agape love. A loving father brings discipline based on vision for their life. So my question to us now is, how do we raise good children? If children refuse the discipline, they are refusing love. If they refuse the love that is connected to discipline, they are like an illegitimate children. Not only is there responsibility for the father to give, but the child must know how to receive. When we cast off the restraints God has placed in our lives, we start drifting without vision. Proverbs 29:18 (KJV) says, *"Where there is no vision, the people perish." Perish* in this context means they will drift away like a ship without an anchor.

When I was 15 years old, I told my mom I would be spending the night at my friend's house, which was not uncommon. It was unusual for my dad to weigh in on those communications with my activities. My mother was the one I would let know what was happening. About 10 o'clock that evening, my friend told me that my dad was on the phone. When I answered, Dad said, "You need to come home." I tried to tell him to check with mom about my plans, but his voice was stern, though normally it wouldn't have been an issue.

When I returned home and walked in, he was standing behind the door with a belt in his hand. He tried to swat me. I reacted and grabbed the belt and jerked it out of his hand and said, "I think I am too big for that anymore." My first thought was, *I shouldn't have said that, now I'll be picking myself up from the floor.* But, he just looked at me with hurt in his eyes, and all he said to me was, "Go on to bed."

All night I felt so badly, but couldn't figure out why. I was feeling like I had done something wrong, yet I knew it had been a misunderstanding. Finally, it came to me why I was feeling like the perpetrator. I had rejected my dad from being a father to me and bringing correction even though it was misunderstood. I felt distant from my father like never before. I couldn't wait till the next morning when I would see him at breakfast. He was a good dad, and it took me by surprise what had happened.

At breakfast I said to him, "I'm sorry for the way I acted last night." He nodded and smiled, and I felt the weight of the whole world lift from me. As mentioned in Chapter 2, some people prefer to be right than righteous, being a right fighter just prolongs the process by arguing the point of who is right or wrong. The bigger issue when it comes to discipline from God the Father is submission to His conviction, which is a way of acknowledging His lordship.

We are either submitting to the father of lies, justifying our sin and feeling depressed, or we submit to the Father of glory and have joy restored. I have witnessed countless couples during counseling sessions waste time by being right fighters; and in some cases, nothing gets resolved because of stubbornness. One night of feeling like an orphan was enough for me. The lessons of so many years ago still carry over with me in keeping a clear conscience of allowing the Holy Spirit to be the first to prick my heart with conviction. When was the last time you felt the correction of your loving Father?

Loving discipline truly is a confirmation that we are still connected to His inner voice. One final thought: just remember, you are sowing into a heavenly account that pays great dividends on earth to carry out the mission you have been called toward. Remember everything we do here will be compensated in eternity. It excites me to know that what

I do now will have eternal rewards that far exceed beyond what I can imagine, but I like to try.

> *Father God, we give praise to You for Your mercy and justice toward us. Our trust and confidence are in You, knowing You keep good books, and it has been accounted in righteousness toward us* (Romans 4:22 NIV).

> *And I saw the dead, great and small, standing before the throne, and books were opened. Another book was opened, which is the book of life. The dead were judged according to what they had done as recorded in the books* (Revelation 20:12 NIV).

> *Lord, help us to be conscious of the truth that You have placed eternity in our hearts to fulfill all that You have written in our book of potentiality.*

> *He has made everything beautiful in its time. He has also set eternity in the human heart; yet no one can fathom what God has done from beginning to end* (Ecclesiastes 3:11 NIV).

> *Amen!*

About
KERRY KIRKWOOD

K ERRY KIRKWOOD is the founding pastor of Trinity Fellowship in Tyler, Texas. He and his wife, Diane, have four children and eight grandchildren. Kerry is known for a strong prophetic anointing. In conjunction with being a senior pastor, Kerry is also the director of Antioch Oasis Network of churches and ministries. He has appeared numerous times on Sid Roth's *It's Supernatural* TV program. He has authored six books and is known as a "pastor to pastors."

In the Right Hands, This Book Will Change Lives!

Most of the people who need this message will not be looking for this book. To change their lives, you need to **put a copy of this book in their hands.**

Our ministry is constantly seeking methods to find the people who need this anointed message to change their lives. **Will you help us reach these people?**

Extend this ministry by sowing 3 books, 5 books, 10 books, or more today, and become a life changer! Your generosity will be part of catalyzing the Great Awakening that many have been prophesying and praying for.

YOUR
Prophetic
COMMUNITY

Sign up for **FREE** Subscription to the Destiny Image digital magazine, and get awesome content delivered directly to your inbox!

destinyimage.com/signup

Sign-up for Cutting-Edge Messages that Supernaturally Empower You

· Gain valuable insights and guidance based on biblical principles
· Deepen your faith and understanding of God's plan for your life
· Receive regular updates and prophetic messages
· Connect with a community of believers who share your values and beliefs

Experience Fresh Video Content that Strengthens Your Prophetic Inheritance

· Receive prophetic messages and insights
· Connect with a powerful tool for spiritual growth and development
· Stay connected and inspired on your faith journey

Listen to Powerful Podcasts that Equips You for God's Presence Everyday

· Deepen your understanding of God's prophetic assignment
· Experience God's revival power throughout your day
· Learn how to grow spiritually in your walk with God

From

Kerry Kirkwood

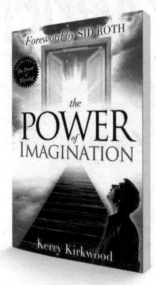

Just imagine!

Does God want you to use your imagination? Are Christians to turn off their imaginative, creative side when they become mature believers? The answers may surprise you!

The Power of Imagination reveals the part of spiritual life that is often shunned or closeted away because it may seem New Age or too unconventional. On the contrary, when believers use their imaginations to see beyond current circumstances into the realm where God paints pictures in their minds, healings are commonplace, goals are accomplished, dreams come true, and victories are celebrated! *But we all, with unveiled face, beholding as in a mirror the glory of the Lord, are being **transformed into the same image from glory to glory, just as from the Lord, the Spirit*** (2 Corinthians 3:14-18).

You can develop the ability to see as God sees. You can see the future that He planned for you before you were born. Through the power of your God-given imagination, nothing is impossible—no problem too big, no relationship too broken. This exciting new way of living is thoughtfully and biblically presented in a refreshing and empowering way that will keep you imagining for years to come.

Purchase your copy wherever books are sold

From

Kerry Kirkwood

The Power of Blessing is more than an encouragement to bless. It shows you many ways you can be a blessing to those around you. Blessings are not just about materialism, blessings are more about a lifestyle that changes environments and conditions among families, churches, communities, and even small businesses and large corporations.

Do not repay evil with evil or insult with insult, but with blessing, because to this you were called so that you may inherit a blessing (1 Peter 3:9 NIV).

Your heavenly Father is the redemptive God who delights in bringing things back into His divine order. Through learning how to bless, you can participate in this redemptive process. By actively living a lifestyle of blessing, you will see changes in the hearts of those you bless—as well as in yourself!

Purchase your copy wherever books are sold

From

Kerry Kirkwood

Let the Holy Spirit Transform Your Thoughts

Is your life everything you would like it to be? Do you feel like you are fulfilling your destiny or do you constantly fight against thoughts of condemnation, fear, hopelessness, or self-doubt?

Many quote the Bible proverb, As a man thinks, so is he. Your thoughts direct your words, shape your future, and ultimately determine your destiny. Kirkwood shows you how to let go of destructive thought patterns and exchange them for life-producing thoughts!

Access the power of right thinking to transform your body, soul, and spirit!

Purchase your copy wherever books are sold

From

Kerry Kirkwood

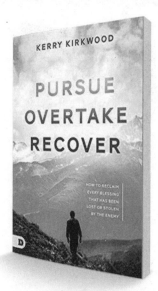

It's Time to Reclaim Everything That's Been Lost or Stolen!

Many Christians understand that Jesus redeemed them from their sins, and because of this, they are right with God. But there is more...much more! Redemption is not just a ticket into Heaven. The redemptive work of Jesus brings restoration, healing, and recovery in every area of your life that has been broken or damaged!

Kerry Kirkwood is a pastor and revelatory writer whose passion is to help believers access the secret power of their redemptive privileges in God.

Get ready to pursue your divine inheritance, overtake your enemy, and recover every promise and provision Jesus made available to you!

Purchase your copy wherever books are sold